Electronics Technology

Also available from Stanley Thornes (Publishers) Ltd

A FIRST ELECTRONICS COURSE   R. B. Arnold

INFORMATION GRAPHICS   Bryan Purves

Electronics Technology

Neil Usher

Hollyfield School, Surbiton

Stanley Thornes (Publishers) Ltd

First published in 1989 by:
Stanley Thornes (Publishers) Ltd
Old Station Drive
Leckhampton
CHELTENHAM GL53 0DN
England

British Library Cataloguing in Publication Data

Usher, N.
    Electronics technology
    1. Electronics. For schools
    I. Title
    537.5

ISBN 0-85950-822-6

Typeset by Tech-Set, Gateshead, Tyne & Wear.
Printed and bound in Great Britain at The Bath Press, Avon.

Contents

Preface

This book is intended mainly for pupils who are following GCSE courses in Electronics, Physics and Technology. The principal aim has been to provide a text which is accessible to a wide range of pupils, rather than to cover the full requirements of any particular published syllabus.

The book can be used in a variety of ways:

1 A **'traditional' approach,** with a Control Technology or Electronics class, might involve teaching most of the Information bank (taking about twenty weeks with an average ability group) before beginning any project work. But even with this approach the book offers the teacher considerable flexibility, since apart from the chapter sequences 2, 3, 4 and 8, 9, 10 the chapters can be taken in almost any order.

2 At the other extreme a teacher operating within a modular curriculum may choose a totally **project-based approach**. One or more of the early projects can be chosen, specifications considered, and only those chapters that are vital to the project need be studied before pupils get down to the business of development followed by building.

3 Teachers who are following a pure **systems approach** will find that Chapters 1, 2, 3 and 4 provide basic training material that leads directly into a wide range of project work. Project 10 is an example of a major project that could remain at the computer-controlled mechanisms level. Other project descriptions and end-of-chapter questions should provoke ideas for further projects.

4 **Physics teachers** will find material appropriate to their courses easily identifiable. For example, the electronics requirements of NEA and MEG Physics are covered in Chapters 1, 5, 7, 9, 11, 12 and 13. Teachers who are new to teaching electronics should find here plenty of assistance for them to create a six or seven week module which meets their examination requirements. Prototype boards are not necessary for the 'physics' sections but they can make certain investigations easier, and pictorial drawings have always been provided where physics classes might want to use them.

5 Chapters 5 and 6, and projects 1 and 2 could be used with 12–14 year olds. Experience with mixed ability classes over the last few years has shown that pupils of this age can work successfully with prototype board, and can build successfully on stripboard without previous soldering experience. The craftwork involved is particularly attractive to boys and girls alike, and it is not unduly expensive. (For example, project 1 at 1989 prices costs about £2.)

Neil Usher
1989

Acknowledgements

I should like to record my gratitude to:

Dr R. A. Haslett of Jaguar Cars for providing so much technical information.

Nick Swift of Griffin & George for lending me an Interpack 2.

David Palmer of DCP Microdevelopments for advice on programs for ZX and IBM machines.

H. M. Lloyd of Deltronics for advice on programs for RML machines.

Joseph Leisten for introducing me to MOSFETs and providing advice on various aspects of practical electronics.

Professor A. K. Som who at the University of Malawi first pressed me into teaching electronics.

Gill Pickup who fought with me in my early years at Hollyfield School.

The pupils of Hollyfield School who have been the guinea pigs for much of the material.

Deb Heighes and Chris Skipp who have made valuable suggestions during the production of the manuscript.

Professor J. A. L. Leisten who has influenced my teaching more than anyone else, and was a constant source of inspiration and support for many years.

My wife who as a basic skills and electronics teacher helped me to evolve teaching techniques that work, and who has made inspiration and the writing task possible.

The author and publisher are grateful to the following:

Hollyfield School for allowing photographs to be taken (pp. 20, 23, 24, 30, 31, 64, 65, 67, 85, 86, 102, 103, 109, 171).

Philips Electronics for providing the photograph on p. 74.

Comet for allowing the photograph to be taken for p. 75.

Jaguar for allowing photographs to be taken for p. 78 and the cover.

IBM for providing the photograph on p. 89.

Research Machines for providing the photograph on p. 89.

Jacquie Gaze of R S Components for providing the photographs on pp. 134, 145, 146, 167, 171.

David Palmer of DCP Microdevelopments for providing an Interpack 2 for the photograph on p. 86.

Mr E J Young of Lock International for providing components for the photographs on pp. 65 and 67.

Janet Mansfield of Omega Electronics for providing components for the photographs on pp. 64 and 66.

Rapid Electronics for providing the component for the photograph on p. 35.

Jane Howard of Jones PR for providing a flag cell and information on Ever Ready batteries.

Alan Miers of Cheltenham College for his help in setting up the systems on pp. 64, 65, 66 and 67.

David Richards for providing the components on pp. 74, 84, 134 and 164.

Section 1

Projects

Ideas for other projects

Choosing a project

1 Do not be too ambitious. It is better to finish a small project than to half-finish a big one.

2 Do not feel that you have to build a complete structure. A robot arm, for example, could be a very big project. You can obtain full marks in an examination for enough good work on just one aspect of the problem, e.g. the 'hand'. (Can you make a hand that 'knows' when something is present and will grip it firmly, but not too firmly?)

However, your title and specifications must describe exactly what you hope to achieve.

3 Think of a possible title and some rough specifications before you look at project books or project ideas in magazines. If you start with an article that provides a solution, you are likely to find very little scope for development work that you can manage.

4 This book contains hints for very many projects.
(**a**) A group of eighteen pupils were asked to read Project 4 and work out a title and specifications for their own work. Four different projects emerged, and there are other possibilities.
(**b**) Many of the problems and questions in the information bank will give you ideas **if you are on the lookout for them in the first place**. For example, the light-seeking structure in Chapter 4 of Section 2 could lead to a variety of electronic and mechanical problems, depending upon the specifications which you write. (Could you use a light beam to direct a jet of water, and even switch the jet on and off? Could you arrange it so that the torch did not move but the receiver rotated from side to side in a fixed arc and the beam was used to latch it in position and later set it moving again?)

5 Do not attempt to build anything that is already mass-produced. For example, any digital clock that you build will be very poor value for money compared with a mass-produced clock.

6 Avoid circuits that you cannot understand. If they do not work when you build them, you will not be able to correct faults in any logical manner. Remember that fault-finding and thorough testing nearly always take more time than building, even when you can understand the circuit.

Writing specifications: an example

Title: Museum security system

An object in a museum requires a mount which triggers an alarm if anyone tries to move the object.

Specifications

1 The alarm must sound when the weight on the museum mount changes by more than 0.5 N.

2 If the force on the mount returns to its original value, the alarm should stay on.

3 It must be possible to alter the weight under which the system operates for any chosen value between 1 N and 20 N.

4 The alarm sound must be a pulsating tone whose frequency rises steadily from 300 Hz to 1 kHz in 1 s before repeating the cycle.

5 The alarm sound must be at least 80 dB at a distance of 1 metre from the loudspeaker.

6 The system must operate from a 9 V d.c. mains power supply unit with maximum output current of 1 A.

7 The circuitry must be fixed rigidly in a sealed box.

8 The weight sensor must be in, or part of, a separate black housing which is approximately 1 cm high, and 10 cm square or 10 cm in diameter.

9 The electrical connection between the two units should be such that any disconnection would trigger the alarm.

Notice:
- Specifications are **numbered sentences**.
- The sentences state what the system must **do** and how it should be presented.
- Each sentence gives **precise information**.

Developing the prototype: general instructions

1 You must first draw a block diagram for your system.

2 If you have access to a kit of manufactured units as used in Chapter 1 of the Information bank, it may be worth using it to help you to obtain the correct block diagram. But beware of the pitfalls. Some buzzers cannot be driven directly by a logic gate, and bistable (latch) units may be NAND gate units (see p. 135).

3 Once you have completed your block diagram, draw the equivalent circuit diagram. Include as much detail about component values as you can. Your block diagram may be wrong and your circuit diagram may be wrong. However, you must draw both diagrams before you attempt to build anything.

Always build from a circuit diagram.

4 Build **one** part of the circuit, corresponding to one of the blocks in the block diagram. Test it. If it does what you want it to do, proceed to the next block.

If any block fails to do what you want it to do, find out why and correct your circuit before going on to the next block. Be prepared to rethink your entire system at each stage of development.

Most important of all, keep a record of every circuit module that you build and of every test that you make. In your final report the record of your failures is as important as the record of your successes.

Report on the final product: general instructions

1 Go through your original list of specifications one at a time and state how well your final product matches your original intentions. If you had to change the specifications in any way, describe the changes and say why you made them.

2 Describe all the cases that you seriously considered using and the reasons for your final choice.

3 Describe how the various parts of the assembly are fixed to the case.

4 Describe any other significant features that are special to your project.

5 If possible support your description with a photograph of the product and another showing the arrangement inside the case.

6 Record any useful thoughts you might have on improving the product and marketing it.

Summary of design information

Resistor colour code

0	black		
1	brown		
2	red	M	= mega = 1 000 000
3	orange	k	= kilo = 1000
4	yellow		
5	green		
6	blue	2k7	= 2700 ohms
7	violet	1M5	= 1 500 000 ohms
8	grey		
9	white		

For how to use the code, see p. 106.

The common colour-coded values are:

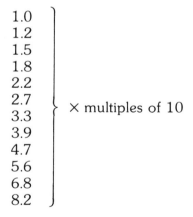

1.0
1.2
1.5
1.8
2.2
2.7
3.3
3.9
4.7
5.6
6.8
8.2
} × multiples of 10

Switches

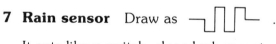 or ──o⁄── is the standard symbol for a switch that is normally open. (Use ──o⁄▲── for relay contacts.)

1 Press-button Can be NO, NC, changeover or latched (i.e. press to close, press again to open).

2 Microswitches Can be operated by button, lever or roller arm. They need only light pressure so can be used to switch a circuit when two objects touch each other.

3 Pressure-pad A simple arrangement to go under a carpet can be home-made.

4 Mercury tilt switch Whether it is open or closed depends upon the orientation of the switch.

5 Liquid-level Two bare wires dipping into the liquid will work as a switch if the liquid is a good enough conductor (see p. 127). Otherwise use a pivoted magnet and reed switch assembly.

6 Magnetic reed switch Draw as  .

7 Rain sensor Draw as 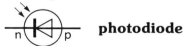 .

It acts like a switch, closed when wet.

Sensors

1 Light

light-dependent resistor

More light makes resistance lower.

photodiode

Use like an LDR. Connect with n side positive, i.e. reverse-biased (specific application on p. 60).

2 Infra red
Use **infra red diode** or **phototransistor** together with an infra red source (details on p. 61).

3 Ultrasonic

Use **ultrasonic receiver** together with ultrasonic transmitter (details on pp. 57–8).

4 Sound

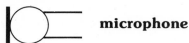

microphone

Sound wave makes resistance of carbon microphone fluctuate (see p. 152).

5 Temperature

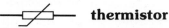

thermistor

Higher temperature makes resistance lower. See also p. 153 on how to use an **ordinary diode** as a temperature sensor. See also **platinum film detector**, p. 45. Also consider **LM335Z** temperature sensor which produces output current proportional to absolute temperature ($1\,\mu$A/K).

6 Position

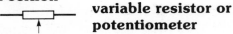

variable resistor or potentiometer

Arm connected to spindle allows movement to be followed (see p. 147).

Input units and initial processing

1 Input units Frequently the first module in a system is one which converts the incoming information into a voltage pattern.

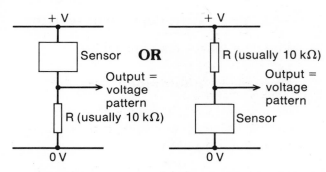

Throughout this book these are called input units. You can use any type of switch or sensor (except ultrasonic) like

this. The position sensor is normally used on its own (see p. 147).

2 To amplify the voltage pattern from an input unit, use an amplifier.

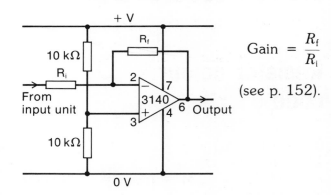

$$\text{Gain} = \frac{R_f}{R_i}$$

(see p. 152).

3 For temperature measurement, see p. 153. **For light level measurement**, see p. 60.

4 The voltage pattern from an input unit is an **analogue** signal. This means that the voltage can have any value between 0 V and +V.

To switch something on and off, the signal must be converted into a voltage pattern which is only high or low. This is called a **digital** signal.

Use a comparator or a logic gate.

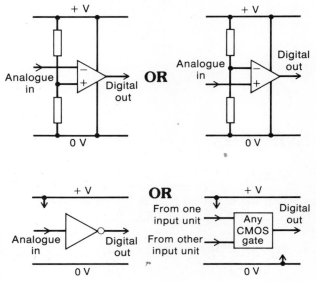

Logic gates

For further information on CMOS ICs, *see CMOS Cookbook*, by Don Lancaster, published by Sams.

1 For inverters (NOT gates) see p. 130.

2 Two-input gates   This is the pin configuration for all CMOS two-input gate ICs.

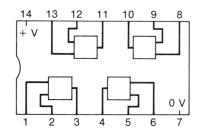

In truth tables 0 stands for low voltage, 1 stands for high voltage.	**4011**	inputs	outputs
		0 0	1
		0 1	1
		1 0	1
	NAND	1 1	0

	4081	inputs	outputs
		0 0	0
		0 1	0
		1 0	0
	AND	1 1	1

	4001	inputs	outputs
		0 0	1
		0 1	0
		1 0	0
	NOR	1 1	0

	4071	inputs	outputs
		0 0	0
		0 1	1
		1 0	1
	OR	1 1	1

	4070	inputs	outputs
		0 0	0
		0 1	1
		1 0	1
	EXCLUSIVE-OR	1 1	0

In practice we often use the NAND gates in a 4011 to make AND and OR gates.
For the AND combination, see p. 125.
For the OR combination, see p. 126.

3 For three-input, four-input and eight-input gates, see *CMOS Cookbook*.

Operating conditions for most CMOS ICs

1 Input   If input voltage $>V/2$ the gate treats it as high. If input voltage $<V/2$ the gate treats it as low. But try to keep the input voltage as close as possible to 0 V or $+V$.

2 Output   Maximum output current is about 10 mA when $+V = 9$ V. For other supply voltages, see *CMOS Cookbook*.

3 Make sure that all unused gates have their inputs connected to 0 V.

Astables

An astable can be used to:
(i)   turn something on and off repeatedly,
(ii) provide clock pulses for a binary counter,
(iii) provide a high frequency waveform for a loudspeaker.

1 Use a 555.

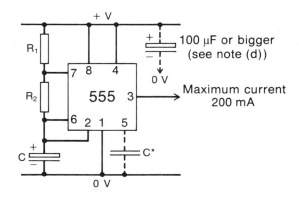

(a)   The circuit generates a 'square wave' voltage pattern.

Time for one cycle (⎍) $= 0.7(R_1 + 2R_2)C$.

This gives the time in seconds if you are using ohms and farads, or megohms and microfarads (see p. 49 for a typical calculation).

(b) Manufacturers recommend that:
  (i) R_1 should not be less than 5 kΩ,
  (ii) R_2 should not be less than 3 kΩ,
  (iii) a 0.01 μF capacitor should be used in the C* position.
  It is needed only when you want very accurate timing and C is a big-value capacitor with significant leakage.

(c) If you disconnect pin 4 from the +V line, it can receive a signal from another module such as a comparator or a logic gate. A high voltage at pin 4 turns the astable on, a low voltage turns it off.

(d) 555 circuits can produce momentary surges of voltage and current on the supply line. These surges can affect the behaviour of logic circuits. To eliminate them, connect a 100 μF capacitor between the +V and 0 V lines, close to pins 8 and 1 of the 555.

2 Use NAND gates (see p. 194) or NOR gates (see p. 58) and *CMOS Cookbook* if you happen to be using a 4011 or 4001 for some other purpose and have two gates spare.

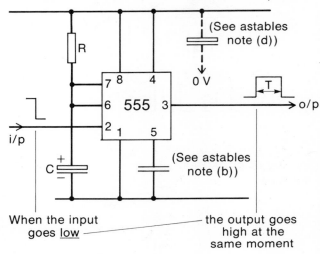

When the input goes high ——— the output goes high at the same moment

2 Use a 555.
Value of $T = 1.1 \times R$ in MΩ $\times C$ in μF.

When the input goes <u>low</u> ——— the output goes high at the same moment

3 To produce a delayed pulse, use two monostables (see p. 138).

Monostables

A monostable can be used to:
 (i) make something keep going for a fixed length of time,
(ii) produce delayed action. (It is easier than using a binary counter which has to be driven by an astable.)

1 Use NOR gates The output stays high for a time T, then it goes low again.

Value of $T = 0.7 \times R$ in MΩ $\times C$ in μF.

Capacitors

1 ——||—— **electrolytic capacitor**
       +   −
Cheapest for large capacitance values and the only type available for very large capacitance values.

2 ——||—— **non-electrolytic** (i.e. all the others)
Ceramic and polyester types are cheapest for general use. For accurate timing control, use tantalum or monolithic ceramic.

3 See also timing note, p. 48.

Bistables

A bistable is also called a flip-flop or a latch.

A bistable can be used to:

(i) keep an output device turned on even when the action that turned it on initially has been reversed,

(ii)

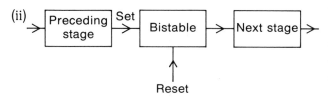

keep the next stage of the system in a particular state even when the output of the preceding stage changes.

1 NOR gate bistable

Whatever happens at the output, the opposite happens at $\overline{Q}$ (assuming set and reset are not both high).

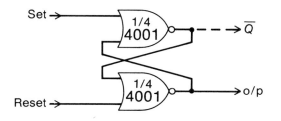

(i) With reset low: when set goes high the output goes high.
(ii) With set returned to low: when reset goes high the output goes low.

2 NAND gate bistable

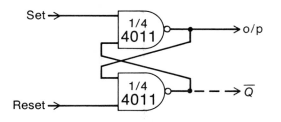

(i) With reset high: when set goes low the output goes high.
(ii) With set returned to high: when reset goes low the output goes low.

Counters

Bit numbers and their values

Bit number	7	6	5	4	3	2	1	0
Denary number	128	64	32	16	8	4	2	1

For examples of conversions, see p. 139.

The main use of a binary counter is to introduce a time delay. This is because the voltage at any output pin goes high some time after the pulses have started to arrive at the clock input.

1 4024 binary counter

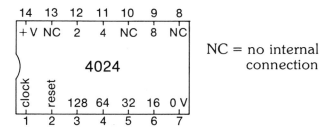

NC = no internal connection

Each time the voltage at pin 1 goes low, the counter advances one count. Reset must be low to allow counting. If the reset goes high all outputs go low.

2 4020 binary counter

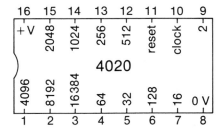

It follows the same rules as a 4024.

3 4017 divide-by-ten counter

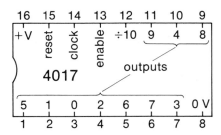

Successive clock pulses make the output pins go high one at a time in the order shown. Useful for running lights and electronic dice. For details see *CMOS Cookbook*.

4 For electromechanical counters, see p. 171.

Protecting the processing units

When a motor or solenoid switches on it can produce a momentary drop of voltage on the positive line. This can affect the behaviour of logic gates. Bistables and counters can be triggered into a different state.

To prevent this from happening:
(1) Put a diode in the positive line between the processing part of the system and the high-power part.
(2) Put a large capacitor between the supply lines, next to the diode.
(3) Take the leads to the power supply from the high-power end of the system.

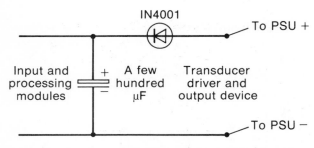

If you are using three or more logic ICs you may need a 0.1 µF capacitor between the supply lines near the supply connections to every third IC.

Using the power equation

You need to calculate the current when you know the power (watts) and the supply voltage.

Example 1 The solenoid of a pneumatic valve is rated at 12 V, 5 W. What is its operating current?

Use **current** $= \dfrac{\textbf{power}}{\textbf{voltage}}$

$= \dfrac{5 \text{ watts}}{12 \text{ volts}}$

$= \underline{0.42 \text{ amps (or 420 milliamps)}}$

Using the Ohm's Law equation

You need to calculate the current when you know the supply voltage and the resistance.

Example 2 A relay coil is rated 5.5–9.9 V, 53Ω. What is its operating current when using a 9 V supply?

Use **current** $= \dfrac{\textbf{voltage}}{\textbf{resistance}}$

$= \dfrac{9 \text{ volts}}{53 \text{ ohms}}$

$= \underline{0.17 \text{ amps (or 170 milliamps)}}$

Calculate the operating currents of the two ultraminiature relays on p. 170.

You have to calculate the resistance that is needed to limit the current at the output of a logic gate.

Example 3 The gate output current must not exceed 10 mA. You want to know the value of R to use.

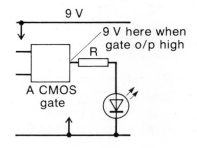

When the LED is on, the p end is about 2 V higher than the n end. Across the resistor the voltage must drop by about 7 V.

Use **resistance** $= \dfrac{\text{voltage}}{\text{current}}$

$$= \frac{7 \text{ volts}}{10 \text{ milliamps}}$$

$$= \underline{\underline{0.7 \text{ kilohms (or 700 ohms)}}}$$

You could use a 680 Ω resistor but it is safer to use 1 kΩ and the LED will be bright enough.

Driving output devices

Maximum output current from:
 (i) 555 = 200 mA
 (ii) 3140 = 6 mA
 (iii) most CMOS ICs = 10 mA when using a 9 V supply.

A transducer driver is needed when the output device needs a bigger current that the final processing unit can supply.

1 Output device current less than 100 mA

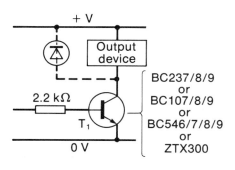

2 Output device current between 100 mA and 1 A

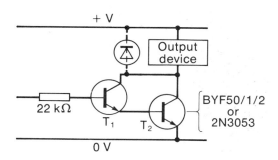

3 Output device current greater than 1 A

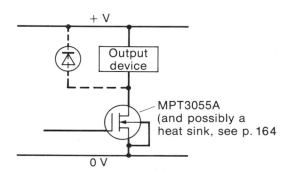

4 If the output device needs a different voltage
Either
 (i) use a **relay**. The relay's solenoid becomes the output device in the transducer driver circuit (see p. 170 for details of relays).
Or
 (ii) use a **MOSFET**.

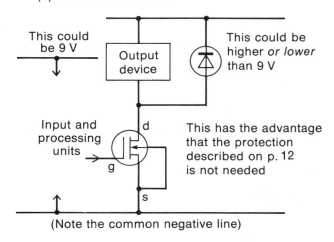

(Note the common negative line)

5 To drive a motor in both directions
use two changeover relays (see p. 170).

Output devices

1 **light-emitting diode**

Standard 5 mm (0.2 inch) LED (red or green or yellow) needs 10 mA for reasonable brightness. When on, p side is 1.7–2.0 V higher than n side. Can be driven directly by CMOS outputs and can therefore be used to monitor them. On 9 V supply use 1 kΩ limiting resistor (or at any rate not less than 680 Ω). On 5 V supply CMOS output is too small to drive an LED to reasonable brightness without damage to CMOS device itself. *See* p. 60 for **ultra bright LEDs**, see p. 61 for **infra red sources**.

2 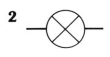 **lamp used as an on-off indicator**

 lamp used to provide illumination

3 Red lead +ve
 d.c. buzzer

A miniature piezo-electric buzzer can be operated on a 9 V supply. The operating current is less than 10 mA. It produces a sound with a fixed frequency which you cannot alter (see p. 35).

4 **loudspeaker**

To produce a sound it needs a continuously varying voltage. For example to produce a sound with frequency 3.4 kHz (the centre frequency of a baby's cry and the frequency at which normal adult hearing is most sensitive) you need to drive it with a 3.4 kHz voltage pattern.

5 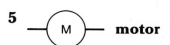 **motor**

6  **relay coil and**

relay contacts

see p. 169 for directional control of a motor.

7 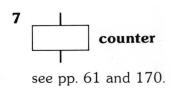 **counter**

see pp. 61 and 170.

8 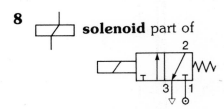 **solenoid** part of

solenoid-operated three-port valve (shown in part of a circuit on p. 171).

Comparison of programming instructions

Output

1 BBC

```
?64705=...   (1 MHz bus)
?65121=...   (printer port)
```

2 RML

```
OUT 29,...
```

3 Spectrum

```
OUT 63,...
```

4 IBM with GW BASIC

```
OUT 769,...
```

Input (with PRINT command)

1 BBC

```
PRINT ?64705 (1 MHz bus)
PRINT ?65120 (User port)
```

2 RML

```
PRINT INP(29)
```

3 Spectrum

```
PRINT IN 63
```

4 IBM with GW BASIC

```
PRINT INP(769)
```

Time delay for one second

1 BBC

```
TIME = 0 : REPEAT UNTIL
         TIME = 100
```

2 RML

```
GET (100)
```

3 Spectrum

```
PAUSE 50   (using 50 Hz mains)
PAUSE 60   (using 60 Hz mains, USA)
PAUSE 80   (using a monitor)
```

4 IBM with GW BASIC

```
FOR T = 1 TO 100 : NEXT T
```

Programs for Acorn BBC machines

Program 1B (see p. 87)

```
10  ?64705 = ... (or ?65121 = ...)
20  TIME = 0 : REPEAT UNTIL
         TIME = n×100
         .
         .                because the clock counts up
         .                to 100 every second
         .
    GOTO 10
```

Program 2B (see p. 88)

```
10  DATA ...
20  READ O, T
30  ? outport address = 0
40  IF T = 0 THEN 70
50  TIME = 0 : REPEAT UNTIL
              TIME = T
60  GOTO 20
70  RESTORE
80  GOTO 10
```

(To recycle a fixed number of times, see p. 91)

Program 3 (see p. 93)

```
10  I = ?64705 (or I = ?65120)
20  IF I = ... THEN ... ELSE ...
30  GOTO 10
```

Programs for RML machines

Program 1B (compare p. 87)

```
10  OUT 29, 15
20  X = GET(200)
30  OUT 29, 60
40  X = GET(400)
50  IF X = 0 THEN 10
60  END
```

This technique is needed because the GET command ignores the ESCAPE key. It simply waits for any key to be pressed during the time specified by the number in brackets.

To stop the program, press any key. (To recycle a fixed number of times, delete lines 50 and 60, and use a FOR ... NEXT loop, see p. 91.)

Program 2A (compare p. 88)

```
1Ø   DATA . . .
2Ø   READ O,T
3Ø   OUT 29,O
4Ø   IF T=Ø OR X<>Ø THEN END
5Ø   X=GET(T)
6Ø   GOTO 2Ø
```

Program 2B (compare p. 88)

```
1Ø   DATA . . .
2Ø   READ O,T
3Ø   OUT 29,O
4Ø   IF T=Ø THEN 7Ø
5Ø   X=GET(T)
6Ø   IF X=Ø THEN 1Ø ELSE 9Ø
7Ø   RESTORE
8Ø   GOTO 1Ø
90   END
```

To stop the program, press any key.

Program 3 (compare p. 93)

```
1Ø   I=INP(29)
2Ø   IF I=247 THEN OUT29,4
     ELSE OUT29,2
3Ø   GOTO 1Ø
```

Line 2Ø assumes the use of an RML version of CONTROL IT or of any other buffer box where the inputs float high.

Program 2A (compare p. 88)

```
1Ø   DATA . . .
2Ø   READ O,T
3Ø   OUT 63,Ø
4Ø   IF T=Ø THEN STOP
5Ø   PAUSE T
6Ø   GOTO 2Ø
```

Program 2B (compare p. 88)

```
1Ø   DATA . . .
2Ø   READ O,T
3Ø   OUT 63,Ø
4Ø   IF T=Ø THEN 7Ø
5Ø   PAUSE T
6Ø   GOTO 2Ø
7Ø   RESTORE
8Ø   GOTO 10
```

To stop the program, press BREAK.

Program 3 (compare p. 93)

```
1Ø   I=IN 63
2Ø   IF I=8 THEN OUT 63,4 ELSE
     OUT 63,2
3Ø   GOTO 1Ø
```

Line 2Ø assumes the use of a Spectrum version of Interpack 2 or of any other buffer box where the inputs float low.

Programs for ZX Spectrum machines

Program 1B (compare p. 87)

```
1Ø   OUT 63,15
2Ø   PAUSE 1ØØ [or 120, or 160, see
                comparison of
                programming
                instructions, p. 15]
3Ø   OUT 63,6Ø
4Ø   PAUSE 2ØØ [or 240, or 320]
5Ø   GOTO 1Ø
```

To stop the program, press BREAK.
(To recycle a fixed number of times, see p. 91.)

Programs for IBM PC/AT/XT machines that are fitted with GW basic

Program 1B (compare p. 87)

```
1Ø   OUT 769,15
2Ø   FOR T=1 TO 2ØØ : NEXT T
3Ø   OUT 769,6Ø
4Ø   FOR T=1 TO 4ØØ : NEXT T
5Ø   GOTO 1Ø
```

To stop the program, press ESCAPE.
(To recycle a fixed number of times, see p. 91.)

Program 2A (compare p. 88)

```
1Ø  DATA ...
2Ø  READ O,T
3Ø  OUT 769,O
4Ø  IF T=Ø THEN END
5Ø  FOR X=1 TO T: NEXT X
6Ø  GOTO 2Ø
```

Program 2B (compare p. 88)

```
1Ø  DATA ...
2Ø  READ O,T
3Ø  OUT 769,O
4Ø  IF T=Ø THEN 7Ø
5Ø  FOR X=1 TO T: NEXT X
6Ø  GOTO 2Ø
7Ø  RESTORE
8Ø  GOTO 1Ø
```

To stop the program, press ESCAPE.

Program 3 (compare p. 93)

```
1Ø  I = INP(769)
2Ø  IF I=8 THEN OUT 769,4
    ELSE OUT 769,2
3Ø  GOTO 1Ø
```

Line 2Ø assumes the use of an IBM version of Interpack 2 or of any other buffer box where the inputs float low.

How the same set of pins can be used to send signals or receive them

is a **tristate buffer**.

When ENABLE is high, o/p follows i/p, i.e. high i/p gives high o/p and vice versa.

When ENABLE is low, o/p is disconnected from the buffer. It will adopt the voltage of whatever it is connected to.

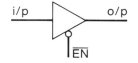

is also a tristate buffer, but o/p can only follow i/p when $\overline{\text{ENABLE}}$ is low.

INTERPACK 2 uses tristate gates on each of the eight input and six output lines.

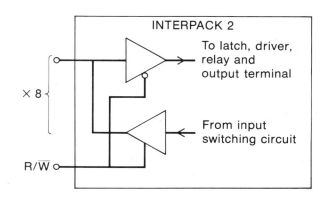

```
?647Ø5      (BBC)
INP(29)     (RML)
IN63        (ZX)
INP(769)    (IBM)
```
puts a high voltage on the $R/\overline{W}$ pin. Information can be 'read', i.e. it can flow from the input sockets to the computer.

```
?647Ø5=     (BBC)
OUT29,      (RML)
OUT63,      (ZX)
OUT769,     (IBM)
```
puts a low voltage on the $R/\overline{W}$ pin. Information can be 'written', i.e. it can flow from the computer to the output circuitry.

Bath water level alarm

This project requires knowledge of Chapters 5 and 6 of Section 2.

The problem

Most people in the UK bath regularly. The bath has to be filled to an appropriate level. Sometimes you need to be doing other things while the bath is filling. This is particularly true if you are running the water for a child or if you are in a hurry to go out. It is inconvenient if you have to keep going back to see how full the bath is.

You are required to design and make an alarm which sounds when the water in a bath reaches the required level. The device must be safe and easy to use, and it must work well and be attractive to look at.

Preparing the specifications

1. The device must be run from a battery, not from the mains. Why?

2. Do you want the battery or power supply unit to be big or small?

3. A bleeping alarm is more effective than one which is on continuously. How many bleeps per second might be most effective?

4. The water level detector includes a pair of long wires. (See the following page.) These wires have to be held straight. How? In a tube? Or can you think of a different method?

Water level detector for bath water level alarm

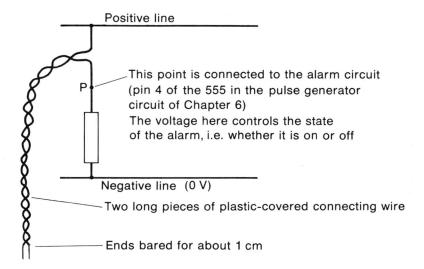

Positive line

P

This point is connected to the alarm circuit
(pin 4 of the 555 in the pulse generator
circuit of Chapter 6)
The voltage here controls the state
of the alarm, i.e. whether it is on or off

Negative line (0 V)

Two long pieces of plastic-covered connecting wire

Ends bared for about 1 cm

The two long pieces of connecting wire act as a switch. When the bared ends dip into
the bath water, the switch is closed, current can flow and the voltage at P is high,
though not as high as the positive line voltage.

When the bath water does not reach the bared ends, the switch is open and P is at
zero volts.

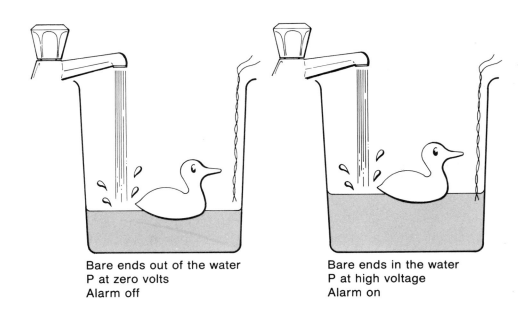

Bare ends out of the water
P at zero volts
Alarm off

Bare ends in the water
P at high voltage
Alarm on

5 You might be able to fit everything except the pair of long wires into a small tin or jar or plastic container. What should the finished article look like? Think of the person to whom you may give it, and the decor of the bathroom.

6 How should the device be attached to the bath?

Having made your decisions, write your **specifications**. This is just a list of your decisions written out clearly so that another person could build the device to your requirements. Include a fully labelled drawing of what you expect the final product to look like.

Developing the prototype

You should have decided on the number of bleeps per second that you require.

The circuit to use is the pulse generator in Chapter 6 of Section 2 with one wire removed so that it can be controlled by the water level detector. Before building it as a soldered circuit you have to consider two more questions:

(1) What values of R_1, R_2 and C are needed to produce your required number of bleeps per second?
(2) What is the best resistor value to use in the water level detector?

To find answers to these questions you must

● build the circuit on prototype board,
● make appropriate measurements on what you have built,
● change component values until further tests provide the results that you need.

Making appropriate measurements

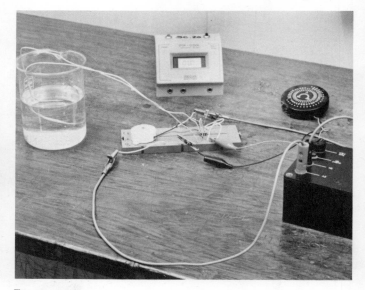

The apparatus

First prepare a table so that all your measurements can be recorded.

Developing the Prototype

Data Required Number of Bleeps per second =

∴ Time That 20 Bleeps Should Take =

	R_1	R_2	C	Measured Time for 20 Bleeps
1				
2				
3				

The component values that I intend to use are R_1 =
R_2 =
C =

Build the basic pulse generator circuit using

R_1 = 10 kΩ

R_2 = 1 MΩ

C = 1 µF or 2.2 µF

(The stepped variable resistor shown in the photograph on p. 20 is useful in the R_2 position.)

Carry out your investigations until the circuit works as required.

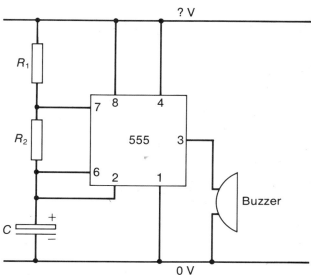

Remove the wire that connects pin 4 to the positive line and add the water level detector circuit, which consists of R_3 and the pair of long wires that were described on p. 19.

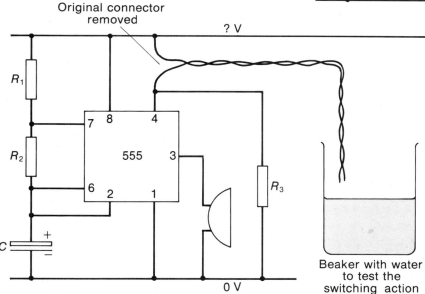

Beaker with water to test the switching action

Start with R_3 very big (1 MΩ or 100 kΩ?) and gradually reduce it until you find **the biggest value of R_3 for which the buzzer is off when the wires do not dip into the water**. Record the value that you have found. To be certain that your final alarm will work correctly, **choose the next smaller resistance value for R_3**.

Stripboard layout for the bath water level alarm circuit

The arrangement of copper strips on a stripboard is different from the
pattern of connections inside a prototype board. This requires the
components to be arranged differently in order to produce the same
circuit.

The bath water level alarm circuit can be built on a piece of stripboard
consisting of nine copper strips, each strip having fifteen holes.

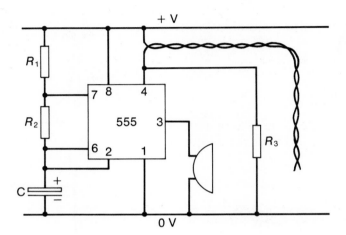

The circuit diagram

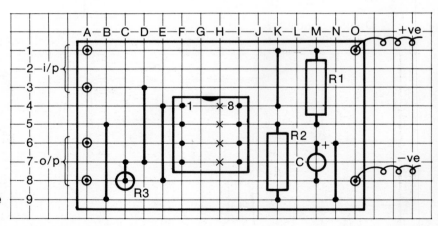

The stripboard layout (seen from the
side without the copper strips)

The stripboard layout can be drawn on ordinary squared paper, which has
5 mm (0.2 inch) squares. The drawing is then twice as big as the actual
arrangement. This is a good idea because it is easier to draw and to follow
the bigger drawing.

You have to imagine that there is a hole wherever two lines of the
squared paper cross. Also imagine that **the copper strips run along the
numbered rows** so that, for example, all the holes in row 3 are connected
to each other.

Check your understanding of the layout drawing.

1 Pin 1 of the IC is connected into hole 4F. Which hole is used for pin 6 of the IC?
2 Is pin 1 of the IC connected to pin 2?
3 What do you think the four crosses on column H represent?
4 Which row of holes is being used for the negative line?
5 Which two wires and which pieces of copper strip connect pin 2 to pin 6?
6 Is the positive terminal of the capacitor connected to pin 2? If so, how?
7 Is pin 1 of the IC connected to R_3? If so, how?
8 Is the positive terminal of the capacitor connected to R_1? If so, how?
9 Eventually, what should be connected to the two terminal pins labelled o/p?
10 Eventually, what should be connected to the two terminal pins labelled i/p?

The soldered circuit

Follow the instructions in Chapter 15 of Section 2.

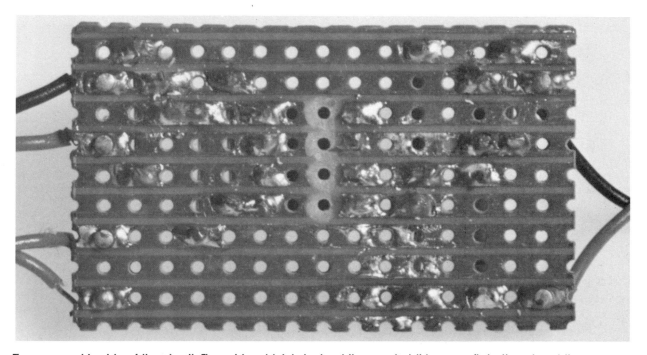

The copper strip side of the circuit. The soldered joints look a bit messy but this was a first attempt and the completed assembly worked well. It is a good idea to practise soldering on a spare piece of board before working on your circuit

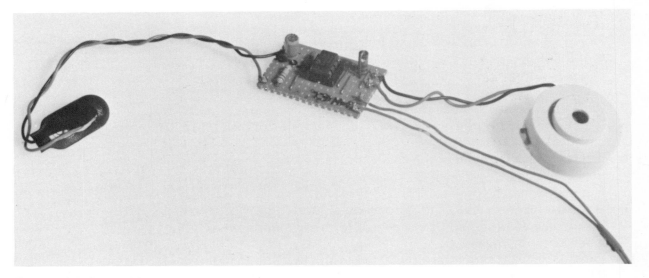

The completed assembly

The container

1 The circuit and a small battery can fit into a cocktail stick container. The buzzer can be fixed to the outside.

Do you want to use the smallest possible container or would you prefer to use a bigger one? Write down what you think are the advantages and disadvantages of each.

2 You may need to use a car touch-up spray or model paint to produce a professional finish. Think of the bathroom where it will be used. Find out what types of paint are available and the relative advantages and disadvantages of each. Record your findings.

3 Decide upon the tube that you will use for the wires. How will you fix it to the case rigidly and with a watertight seal?

4 How will it be held in position?

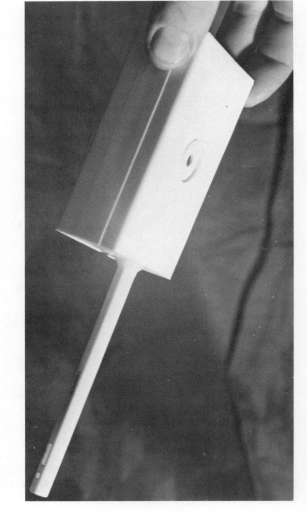

A Christmas present that gave a lot of satisfaction to its maker and which is used frequently in its new home. Notice the small holes near the bottom of the tube

Fixing things inside it

1 If you are using a small container it may be possible to fit things in tightly, perhaps with the help of some packing material. In a larger container things will have to be fixed in place.

Consider all the adhesives that may be useful as well as pipe clips and all the other common fixing aids. A visit to a DIY shop might be useful. Make notes about some of the possibilities you consider. Say why you reject some and favour others.

2 If you are fixing things in place, consider ease of servicing if a fault develops or a battery needs replacing. Having the stripboard fixed to the case and a buzzer or battery connected to the lid can cause problems.

3 The bath alarm circuit will cause a slow continuous power drain from the battery, even when the circuit is not on. If the circuit is not used very often it may be necessary to make the battery easily removable. Alternatively, incorporate a miniature rocker switch in one of the battery leads.

Report on the final product

1 Go through your original list of specifications, one at a time, and state how well your final product matches your original intentions. If you had to change the specifications in any way, describe the changes and say why you made them.

2 Describe all the cases and tubes that you seriously considered using and the reasons for your final choices.

3 Describe how the various parts of the assembly are fixed to the main case.

4 Describe any other significant features of the final product, such as method of support, tube drainage and decoration.

5 If possible, support your description with one photograph showing the product and another showing the arrangement inside the case.

6 Record any useful thoughts you might have on marketing the product.

Timer for times up to twenty minutes

This project requires knowledge of Chapters 5 and 6 of Section 2.

The problem(s)

Some foods need cooking for an exact length of time. Examples are soft-boiled eggs, biscuits and small cakes. It is useful to have a timer that sounds an alarm when the right time has passed.

A timer would also be useful in some games like Trivial Pursuit® and some hobbies, like photography. These may need short times, maybe less than a minute.

Your task is to design and make a timer that is suitable for one or both of the above situations. It must be safe and easy to use. It must work well and be attractive to look at.

Preparing the specifications

First you must consider the following points and make your own decision about each one.

1 What foods need fairly precise cooking times or preparation times that are less than 20 minutes? Consult the most experienced cook in your family. Make a list and from it decide the shortest and longest times that need measuring.

2 Make a list of other activities where a timer might be useful. For these activities what are the shortest and longest times that need timing?

3 Decide what kind of timer you want to build. How accurate must the timing be? Will an extra 30 seconds make much difference? How about 15 seconds, or 5 seconds?

4 The accuracy of your timer depends on how long the maximum delay is before the alarm sounds. For example, if the longest time is to be 4 minutes, your alarm would be accurate to within 10 seconds of the set time. If you choose a shorter maximum delay, your timer will be more accurate. If you go for a longer maximum delay, it will be less accurate.

Now make your final decisions about timing. What do you intend to aim for as regards shortest time, longest time and accuracy of timing?

5 Your circuit will need to be put in a box with a circular dial in it. You will obtain advice on making the dial later. Decide now what you want the finished box to look like. Think of its possible uses and the person to whom you may give it. Prepare a labelled sketch to show what it might look like.

Finally, under the heading **specifications**, write out a list of your decisions.

Power-up one-shot

This circuit generates a single pulse as soon as you switch the power on. The voltage at pin 3 goes high, stays high for a while, drops to zero volts and stays there. It will not generate another pulse until you have switched off the power supply and switched it on again. This is why it is called a 'power-up one-shot'.

The length of the pulse, i.e. the time that the output voltage is high, is controlled by the resistance of R_1 and the size of the capacitor.

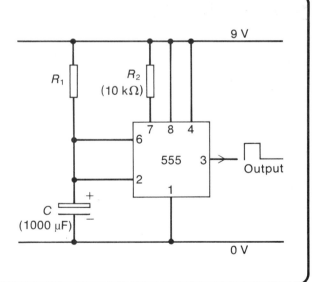

Developing the prototype

1 Build the power-up one-shot circuit using $R_1 = 10 \text{ k}\Omega$, $R_2 = 10 \text{ k}\Omega$, $C = 1000 \text{ }\mu\text{F}$.

2   Switch a testmeter to its 10 V d.c. range. Connect testmeter **+** to pin 3
and **−** to pin 1. When power to the circuit is switched on, the pointer
should immediately jump to positive line voltage, stay there for a little
longer than 10 seconds, drop to 0 V and stay there.

**If your circuit fails to operate correctly, follow the test
procedure on p. 110 before asking for help.**

3   If the circuit works correctly, remove the testmeter. Try the two ways of
connecting a buzzer to the circuits shown below.

Remember to switch off, switch on, and listen for the delay. Decide
which arrangement is the better one to use for your timer.

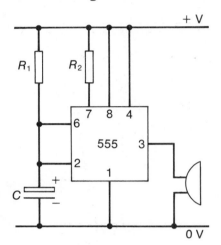 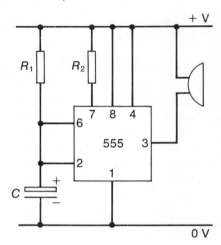

You should have made two decisions which affect the electronic
circuit:
(1)   The longest interval that needs timing. (This circuit is unsuitable
       for times that are longer than 20 minutes if you want to use it for
       a variety of times.)
(2)   The shortest interval that needs timing.

4   Before you can build your soldered circuit you have to find the values
of R_1 that will produce your shortest and longest time intervals.

First prepare a table so that all your measurements can be recorded.

Developing the Prototype

Data

R_1	Measured Time Intervals

Value of R_1 needed for the shortest time =
Value of R_1 needed for the longest time =

Points you may find useful are:
(1)   The time delay varies in proportion to the R_1 values. For
       example, $R_1 = 100 \text{ k}\Omega$ gives a time delay ten times longer than
       $R_1 = 10 \text{ k}\Omega$.

(2)   After switching off, allow at least a minute before switching on again. The capacitor needs time to discharge if you want to obtain reliable time measurements.

(3)   A stepped variable resistor like that shown in the photograph on p. 20 is useful in the R_1 position.

Now carry out your investigations until you have all the information you require.

5   Try out the final version of the circuit which includes a variable resistor as shown here.

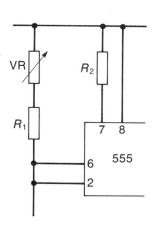

R_1 should have the **smallest** value that you need, i.e. the one that gives the shortest time you will ever want to set.

VR stands for 'variable resistor'. You can change the resistance in the circuit by turning the spindle. By adding the value written underneath it to the value of R_1 you will get the biggest resistance your circuit can have. Choose a variable resistor that will give you the longest time delay you will need.

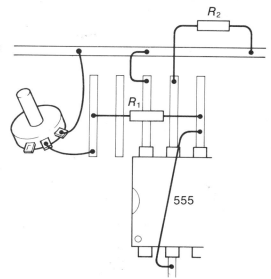

Stripboard layout for the timer circuit

The timer circuit can be built on a piece of stripboard consisting of eight copper strips. Each copper strip needs fifteen holes.

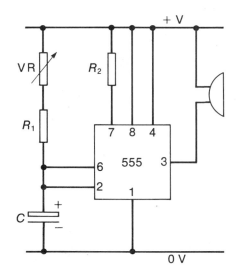

The circuit diagram

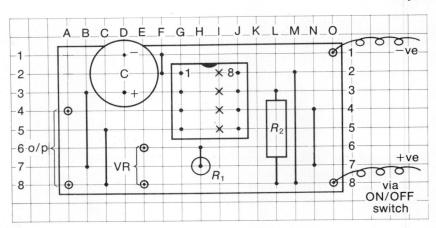

The stripboard layout (seen from the side without the copper strips)

You have to imagine that there is a hole wherever two lines of the squared paper cross. Also imagine that **the numbered rows represent the copper strips**. This means that all the holes in row 7, for example, are connected to each other.

Check your understanding of the layout drawing.

1 Pin 8 of the IC is connected into hole 2J. Which hole is used for pin 4 of the IC?

2 What do the four **x**'s on column I represent?

3 Which row of holes is used for the negative line?

4 Which two wires and which pieces of copper strip connect pin 2 to pin 6?

5 Is the positive terminal of the capacitor connected to pin 6? If so, how?

6 Is one end of R_1 connected to pin 2? If so, how?

7 Is pin 4 connected to pin 8? If so, how?

8 What should eventually be connected to the two terminal pins labelled o/p?

The soldered circuit

Follow the instructions in Chapter 15 of Section 2.

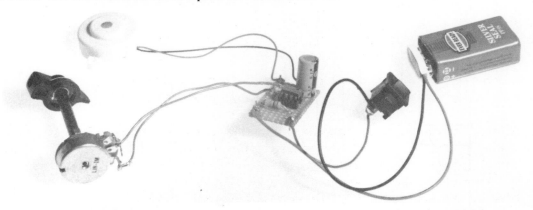

The completed assembly

The container

The finished article could look something like this. The pupil has used an ABS box. Model paint could be used to match a kitchen decor. If all parts of the system are fixed to the lid, servicing is easy. If you do not want to buy a special box, look for a jar or plastic container with a big enough lid

The method of fixing is important (nuts and bolts, or adhesives) because the timer must not be damaged if it falls from a work surface to the floor. You might find a visit to a DIY shop useful for ideas and advice.

To mount a miniature rocker switch you will have to cut out a rectangular hole. First mark out the intended position, then drill small holes round the edge inside the rectangle. The holes should be as close together as possible without touching. Then push the central part through and use a flat or △ file to produce a clean finish.

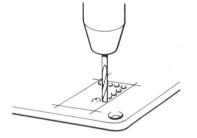

Calibration of the timer

The dial needs a scale, with times marked on it, and a pointer-knob to indicate the times you want to set. Putting the scale and knob on correctly is called **calibrating** the timer. A good looking dial can be made from clear plastic, with transfers of numbers stuck on to it.

You will need to make trials with a stopwatch or stopclock to enable you to position the numbers correctly. This will be a time consuming task.

You may get different time delays when the pointer is at the same setting. This is caused by the capacitor not discharging properly when the circuit is switched off. Solve the problem by adding a switch in parallel with the capacitor. A simple miniature push switch connected by wires to terminal pins at 3A and 1A will do the trick. Press this switch after turning your circuit off.

Consumer information

All operating instructions and other advice to the consumer should be written as clearly and simply as possible. It should not be easy for the owner to lose it. Write out the necessary consumer information and decide how and where to display it.

Report on the final product

1 Go through your original list of specifications one at a time and state how well your final product matches your original intentions. If you had to change the specifications in any way, describe the changes and say why you made them.

2 Describe all the cases that you seriously considered using and the reasons for your final choice.

3 Describe how the various parts of the assembly are fixed to the case.

4 If possible support your written report with a photograph of the product and another showing the arrangement inside the case.

5 Record any useful thoughts you might have on improving the product and on marketing it.

Alarm system for temperature or light level falling too low

This project requires knowledge of Chapters 5, 8 and 11 of Section 2.

The problems

An elderly person, or someone recovering from illness, may need to be warned if the temperature outside the house is below a certain level.

Tropical fish and small mammals need a certain minimum temperature for survival.

Seeds and seedlings need a minimum temperature for growth. They may also require plenty of light.

Many people could find a use for an alarm system which indicated when the temperature or the light level became too low.

Preparing the specifications

1   Decide which particular problem or situation is of most interest to you or to someone you know who might appreciate an alarm system.

2   Decide whether your alarm system has only to detect low temperature or whether it should be triggered if either the **temperature** or the **light level** becomes too low.

3 In some cases the device must **always** be triggered at the **same** temperature. The triggering temperature can then be set by the manufacturer (you) before the device leaves the workshop.

In other cases the user may want to select different temperatures. You would then have to **calibrate** the device, i.e. produce a scale with temperatures marked on it and a pointer knob to allow the desired temperature to be selected.

Decide which type you need to make. Also find out the temperature or range of temperatures it has to work at, and how accurate it needs to be. Will it matter if it is 1°C out? How about 5°C?

4 The circuit could be powered by a battery, with an ON/OFF switch to prevent the battery from running down when the device is not in use. Alternatively it could be powered by one of the mains power supplies that are available for use with home computers. Consider their relative advantages.

5 What should the finished article look like? Consider colour and size, whether it should be fixed in position, whether it needs to be watertight, and anything else that could be important. Prepare a labelled sketch to show what it might look like.

Remember that these considerations can be as important as the electronics in ensuring the commercial success of a product.

When you have made your final detailed decisions, list them under the heading **specifications**.

Developing the prototype

Follow the instructions on p. 5.

1 If you are not interested in the light level, a basic system might go together like this.

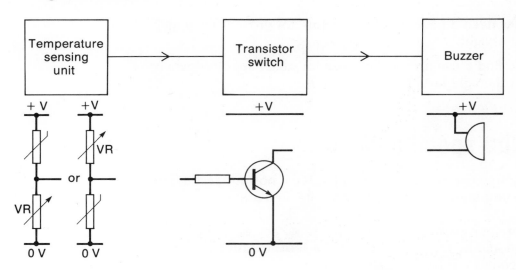

If you try this you may find that the switching action of the circuit does not satisfy you. To improve it you could put a logic gate such as

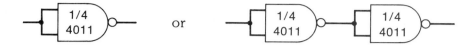

between the temperature-sensing unit and the transistor switch. If you are using a miniature buzzer you could then do without the transistor switch.

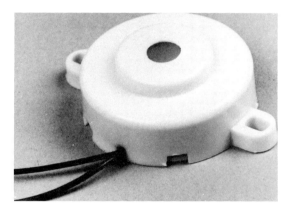

Miniature round piezo-electric buzzer with flying leads. Output is continuous tone, typically 4 kHz with a sound output level of 70 dB at 1 m. Power requirement 12 V d.c. approximately 4 mA.

Details from the catalogue of Rapid Electronics Ltd. The buzzer works well on 9 V d.c. (or 5 V d.c.). The current is about 5 mA (3 mA on 5 V). A CMOS logic gate can source or sink about 10 mA on a 9 V supply (4 mA on a 5 V supply)

2 You change the triggering temperature by turning the spindle of VR. If you are using a gate, the system will trigger when the thermistor's resistance becomes equal to that of VR. You need to know the biggest resistance that your thermistor will have (corresponding to the lowest temperature setting) so that you can select an appropriate VR.

3 If you require the system to be triggered by low temperature OR low light level, make sure that you understand the section 'Using LDRs and thermistors to control gates' in Chapter 11 of Section 2.

You have three choices for producing an OR gate.

4 Follow **all** of the instructions on p. 5 until you have a working prototype and a full record of your development work. Include its **failures** as well as its **successes**.

The soldered circuit

You have to work out the stripboard layout for yourself. Example 4 on
p. 192 should help you. You should plan several arrangements before
settling for one.

When you build the circuit, follow the plan of work in Chapter 15.

Temperature calibration

If your system has to be usable at different temperatures, you must
provide a scale with temperatures marked on it and a pointer knob which
enables times to be selected correctly. A piece of clear plastic with
numbers put on with transfers can look good.

Trials with a thermometer and a way of varying the temperature will be
needed to enable you to position the numbers correctly.

Report on the final product

1   Go through your original list of specifications one at a time and
    state how well your final product matches your original
    intentions. If you had to change the specifications in any way,
    describe the changes and say why you made them.

2   Describe all the cases that you seriously considered using and
    the reasons for your final choice.

3   Describe how the various parts of the assembly are fixed to the
    case.

4   Describe any other significant features that are special to your
    project.

5   If possible support your description with a photograph of the
    product and another showing the arrangement inside the case.

6   Record any useful thoughts you might have on improving the
    product and marketing it.

Water level control

PROJECT 4

This project requires knowledge of Chapters 5, 8, 9, 12 and 14 of Section 2. (Also Chapters 6 and 10 for a timed system.)

The problem

A tray of potted plants needs to have a supply of water, but never too much. The same requirement (a supply, but not too much) applies to the water in bird baths and in the drinking troughs of various animal housings – hutches, pens, stables and so on.

The water can be pumped from reservoirs ranging in size from large jars to water butts. It could be pumped regularly, once every few hours; or it could be pumped when it was needed, when the level was too low or the soil was too dry.

Preparing the specifications

1   Decide which particular situation is of most interest to you or to someone you know who might appreciate an automatic pumping system.

2   The pump could **turn on** regularly, once every few hours or once every day. Alternatively it could come on when the water level is too low or when something has become too dry.

Decide **what** should make your pump turn on.

3   The pump could **turn off** after being on for a fixed length of time. Alternatively it could turn off when the water has reached an upper level or when something has become wet enough.

Decide what should make your pump turn off.

4   A car windscreen washer pump is satisfactory for any of the applications in this project. New ones are not particularly expensive and cheap secondhand ones are readily available.

Such a pump can pump water quite quickly, **too** quickly for some applications. Decide whether you want it to pump at full speed or whether the flow rate needs to be fairly slow.

5   A car or motorcycle battery might be an appropriate power supply for the whole system. If you want a timed system you may prefer to have the electronic part powered separately by one of the mains power supply units that are used with some home computers. The battery can then be taken off the system for recharging without affecting the timing.

6   Consider boxing, fixing, waterproofing and appearance. Prepare a labelled sketch to show what the finished article might look like.

When you have made your final detailed decisions, list them under the heading **specifications**.

Developing the prototype

Follow the instructions on p. 5.

1   Your first task is to work out a block diagram for your system. One of the following might fit or be close to your requirements.

(a)
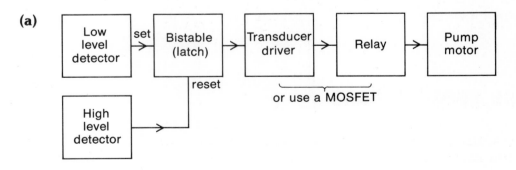

(b)
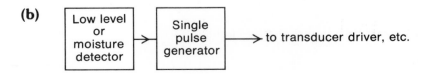

(c)

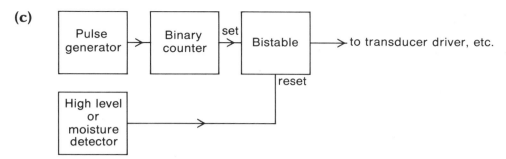

2 Draw the equivalent circuit diagram for each block.

   If you need a **pulse generator** you could use the 555 circuit that is used throughout this book. Alternatively you could use the idea shown on p. 194. $R_1 = 100\ \text{k}\Omega$ and $C = 4.7\ \mu\text{F}$ gives about one cycle per second.

3 Build and test the **input and processing** parts of the circuit. You do not need a transducer driver or a relay or a pump until the earlier parts of the circuit have been built and tested.

4 Next investigate the **pump**. To pump water at the rate you require, what operating voltage is needed and what size electric current flows in the motor? This circuit will provide the answer.

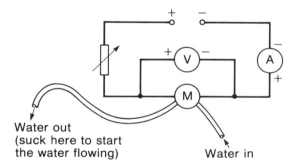

If you have a variable voltage power supply unit, you can do without the variable resistor.

One pump gave the following test results:
- on 12 volts, current = 3 amps,
- on 6 volts, current just under 2 amps,
- on 3 volts, current 1 amp.

Water out
(suck here to start
the water flowing)

Water in

5 When you know the requirements of the pump motor, the driving system can be chosen. Information on some relays and on how to drive them is given on p. 170. Information on MOSFETs is given on pp. 163 and 164.

The soldered circuit

You have to work out the stripboard layout for yourself. Examples 5 and 6 on pp. 193 and 194 should help you.

Report on the final product

Follow the instructions on p. 6.

Automatic door control

Knowledge of Chapters 5, 8, 9, 11, 12 and 13 of Section 2 could be useful in this project.

The problem

Many public buildings now have doors that open when a person approaches. Many lifts have doors that open when a button is pressed or when the lift arrives at its destination. Some garage doors open when a car approaches. Some animal traps have doors that close when an animal has entered. Some homes have curtains that close when a button is pressed. Some offices have blinds that adjust themselves depending upon how sunny it is.

The garage door at your house may not be automatic. The doors or lifts or conveyors on a model railway or warehouse may not be automatic. The doors of the school workshop may be a nuisance or even a hazard to a pupil who has to use a wheelchair. The curtains in your grandparents' living room may be too difficult for them to manage easily.

Your task is to automate a 'door' of your choice.

Preparing the specifications

1   Decide which particular situation is of most interest to you or to someone you know.

2 (a) How is the 'door' operated at present? Is it hinged, sliding, up and over, or pull-cord operated?

(b) If it were automated what could you use to drive it – electric motor or pneumatic valve, with or without gears or levers?

3 How big a force will be needed? You may have to do some force or torque measurements and design your driving mechanism accordingly. If you are considering using a pneumatic system, check that the pressure in the air line multiplied by the piston area gives you a big enough force.

4 Does it matter how quickly the 'door' opens and closes?

5 What action(s) should switch the driving component on? Be as precise as possible about this.

When should it switch off, and what safety precautions should be included?

6 The cheapest way to operate a real garage or workshop door would be to use the mains as your energy source. The only safe way you could do it would be to use a low voltage power supply that plugs into the mains. The options are:

(a) use a low voltage regulated supply for everything, as you probably do in technology lessons anyway,

(b) use a low voltage unregulated supply for the motor and a battery for the electronic control circuits.

7 Consider boxing, positioning and fixing of switches and sensors, control circuitry and wiring. Prepare labelled sketches.

When you have made your final detailed decisions, list them under the heading **specifications**.

Developing the prototype

Follow the instructions on p. 5.

1 Set up the motor or pneumatic system, together with any other mechanical linkages that are necessary. Check that it will drive the 'door'.

If you are using a motor, measure the current and voltage while it is driving the 'door'. This information will enable you to decide upon your choice of a relay and of transistors for the transducer driver (see p. 170).

2 Follow the usual steps in developing the electronic control circuit.

P R O J E C T

6

Quiz game controller (for two teams)

This project requires knowledge of Chapters 5, 7, 8 and 9 of Section 2.

The problem

In some games two teams or two people compete to be first to answer a question. The contestants get the chance to answer by being the first to press their button. Their light comes on and there is a short burst of sound. The control system should prevent the other team's light from coming on until the referee has reset the system.

You have to design and build the complete system.

Preparing the specifications

Begin by listing, in detail and in the correct order, exactly what the system must do. A good way to do this would be in the form of a flowchart.

Add your decisions about what lights to use (red, yellow and green LED's are obtainable), how long the burst of sound should last, and any preferences you may have about the press-buttons, the box(es) and the method of supplying power to the system.

Developing the prototype

Follow the instructions on p. 5.

You will need all of the following blocks, and in some cases more than one of them.

Switch unit	Bistable	Gate	Single pulse generator	Light indicator	Miniature buzzer

Two suggestions:
(1) Make sure that you fully understand the operation of a bistable. Could the output of one bistable be used to prevent another one from working?
(2) To prevent the system from becoming too complicated, you may prefer to use the power ON/OFF switch as the referee's reset switch.

Oven temperature indicator

This project requires knowledge of Chapters 5, 8 and 11 of Section 2.

The problem

After an oven has been switched on it may take quite a long time before it reaches the selected temperature. In most ovens there is nothing to show when the required temperature has been reached. Your task is to design and make a system which can be set to give a signal when any required oven temperature has been reached.

Preparing the specifications

1   The signal could be a visual one from a bulb or an LED, or an audible one from a buzzer. Decide which would be best.

2   Your final practical task will be to **calibrate** the device, i.e. to produce a scale with temperatures marked on it and a pointer knob which enables the correct temperature to be selected. How accurate must it be? Will it matter if it is 1 °C out, or 10 °C, or 30 °C?

3   The circuit could be powered by a battery, with an ON/OFF switch to prevent the battery from being run down when the device is not in

use. Alternatively it could perhaps be powered by one of the mains power supplies that are available for use with home computers. Consider their relative advantages.

4 You will end up with a box that has a circular dial on it. What should the finished article look like? Think of the person to whom you may give it and the cooker with which it may be used. Prepare a labelled sketch to show what it might look like.

When you have made your final detailed decisions, list them under the heading **specifications**.

Developing the prototype

Follow the instructions on p. 5.

The block diagram for the system will follow this pattern.

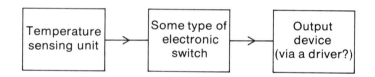

Thermistors cannot be used at high oven temperatures, but you could use a **platinum film detector** (available from RS Components, stock no. 158–238). This has a resistance of 100 Ω at 0 °C and its resistance increases by 0.385 Ω per °C.

The simplest arrangement which might satisfy you is like this.

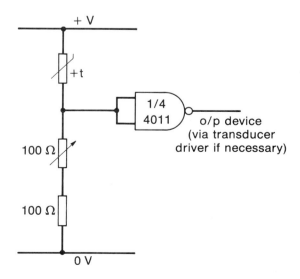

You could also try using a **comparator circuit** (see p. 151).

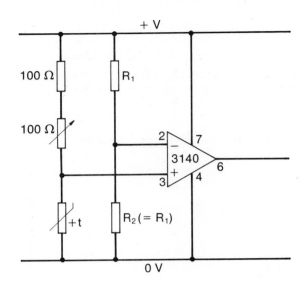

 is an **operational amplifier** (op-amp for short). A 3140 is an 8 pin IC package, like a 555.

Pins 7 and 4 are the positive and negative supply terminals.
Pin 6 is the output terminal.
Pin 2 is the **inverting input** terminal
Pin 3 is the **non-inverting** input terminal.

How it works (see also p. 151).

If the voltage at pin 3 is higher than the voltage at pin 2, the output voltage is almost **+** V. If the voltage at pin 3 is lower than that at pin 2, the output voltage is nearly 0 V.

Timer

This project requires knowledge of most of the Information bank.

The problem

The aim of this project is to produce a multipurpose timer with some or all of the following features:

- a number of ranges so that acceptably accurate delay times can be set from a few seconds to at least a few hours,
- an alternative mode of operation in which the alarm sound is fairly brief and the system automatically repeats the timing process indefinitely,
- a 'hold' facility: when a button is pressed the count is held; on releasing the button (or pressing it again) the count continues,
- alternative ways of starting and/or stopping the timing, e.g. resulting from a change in temperature, light intensity, water level or pressure,
- an output which allows the timer to control an external motor or solenoid.

Preparing the specifications

1   You can probably imagine all sorts of uses for such a device. The list of **likely** uses is much shorter. Begin by making your personal list of possible uses for the device.

2   On the basis of your list, work out what your device needs to do –
shortest and longest times, ranges, accuracy, alternative facilities, alarm
signal(s), power available for driving external devices, how much
circuitry to provide for alternative inputs, and anything else you can
think of.

3   Investigate the availability of switches, sockets, dials and cases and
work out the possible appearance of the final product.

4   Think again about items 1 to 3. Are you being sensible and realistic? If
not, modify your requirements.

5   Write your specifications.

Developing the prototype

Follow the instructions on p. 5.

Your system may be based on the ideas of Chapter 10. Details of ripple
counters can be found in the *CMOS Cookbook* by Don Lancaster,
published by Sams. Note that two 4020s can count up to 16 384 times
16 384, which is a very big number.

To ensure accurate timing you should avoid using an electrolytic or a
ceramic disc capacitor in the pulse generator circuit. The choice will
probably be between solid tantalum and monolithic ceramic, depending
upon availability, cost and capacitance value required.

The following information on the 555 astable (i.e. pulse generator) may be
useful.

$$\text{Time for one cycle} = (R_1 + 2R_2)C$$

This gives the time in seconds if R_1 and R_2 are in ohms and C is in farads.
It would also give the time in seconds if you used megohms with
microfarads.

$$\text{Frequency} = \frac{1}{0.7(R_1 + 2R_2)C} \quad \text{cycles per second}$$

The minimum values for the timing resistors are $R_1 = 5 \text{ k}\Omega$ and $R_2 = 3 \text{ k}\Omega$.
To obtain a linear time scale, the value of R_1 must be much less than that
of the (variable) R_2.

A typical calculation

$$\text{Suppose } R_1 = 10 \text{ k}\Omega \; (= 0.01 \text{ M}\Omega)$$
$$R_2 = 100 \text{ k}\Omega \; (= 0.1 \text{ M}\Omega)$$
$$C = 2.2 \, \mu\text{F}$$

$$\text{Time for one cycle} = 0.7 \, (0.01 + 2 \times 0.1) \, 2.2 \text{ seconds}$$
$$= 0.7 \times 0.21 \times 2.2 \text{ seconds}$$
$$= 0.32 \text{ seconds}$$

$$\text{Frequency} = \frac{1}{0.32} \text{ cycles per second}$$
$$= \underline{\underline{3.1 \text{ cycles per second}}}$$

Automatic porch light

This project requires knowledge of most of the Information bank.

The problem

Many houses have a light in an enclosed front porch, but often the light is not switched on if no visitor is expected. A visitor arriving unexpectedly has to find the bell-push in the dark.

When anyone leaves the house it would be convenient if the porch light stayed on for a while before switching off automatically.

Your task is to devise and make a suitable control system for a porch light.

Preparing the specifications

1 What action(s) should make the porch light turn on – opening the porch door, opening the house door, pressing the bell-push, or some other action?

2 If either door is closed, should the light stay on?

3 What action(s) should make the light turn off?

4 When should the light turn off?

5 Your control system should require very little power, therefore it is reasonable to run it from a battery. Your decision about power supply should be included in your list of specifications.

When you have made your final, detailed decisions covering all possibilities, list them under the heading **specifications**.

Connecting to the mains

Your final task will be to have your completed system connected to the existing porch light switch. Since this means connecting to the mains:
- **it must be done by a qualified electrician,**
- your system must be housed in a **metal** case which must be **earthed,**
- you must use a relay so that there is no direct connection between your control circuit and the mains.

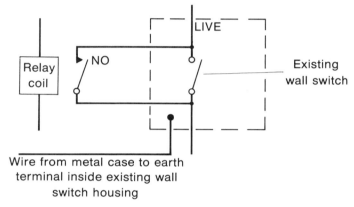

These three safety precautions must be added to your list of specifications.

Developing the prototype

Follow the instructions on p. 5.

You must first draw a block diagram for your system. The most difficult part of this involves the delayed switching off. Question 9 on p. 138 might help to guide your thinking.

There is no need to connect your prototype board circuit to the mains. You will be able to hear whether the relay contact is switching when it should, and a testmeter on a resistance range and connected to the contact terminals will give you any further proof that you require.

Final installation and testing

This must be done by a qualified electrician.

Model for an automatic cattle-feeding system

**Knowledge of Chapters 3 and 4 of Section 2 is necessary.
Knowledge of other chapters will be needed if you intend to
produce any soldered circuitry.**

Some information on cows

Cows are creatures of habit. When a cow has been led to a particular
feeding cubicle for two or three consecutive feeds, it will always return to
that cubicle of its own accord.

Also, if it is given the right amount of food, a healthy cow will eat all of
the food that is supplied. A sick cow will just not come to its cubicle.

The problem

During the winter, cows are fed indoors. Their food could be in the form
of small pellets. Ideally they should eat a fixed quantity of food in every
six-hour period.

Your task would be to build a model of an automatic feeding system for
cows. Your model should operate as far as possible like a commercial
system, except that everything would be on a small scale.

You could choose some other animal if you prefer. You would have to
find out its feeding habits. For a domestic pet you might produce a
working system instead of a model.

Preparing the specifications

1   An automated system might work like this:
    * when a cow appears in its cubicle, a ration of food is delivered,
    * if the cow appears a second time in the same six-hour period, no food is delivered,
    * if a cow misses one six-hour period, a double helping is delivered when it appears during the next six-hour period,
    * if a cow misses two successive six-hour periods, the farmer would receive a warning that the cow is sick.

    You should first try to summarise this sequence in the form of a flowchart. For your model you could use a minute to represent six hours.

2   When you have completed your flowchart (for **one** cow), decide whether you will use a computer based control system during the development period and even for your final submission.

3   Consider the details of the actual food-supply mechanism.
    (a) How much 'food' will your model deliver? What will you use as food? The hopper from which the food is delivered must contain enough for at least four feeds.
    (b) How will your system measure out and deliver fixed amounts of food? Will you use one or two trapdoors operated by solenoid bolts?

    Prepare detailed sketches of different food supply mechanisms, as many as you can. Then select the one which you think that you should try out first.

4   (Only if you can bear the thought of further complications!)
    (a) A slightly sick cow may come into its cubicle but not eat anything. Could you modify your system to cope with this in any way?
    (b) In a commercial system, a cubicle will be used by a number of cows, though only by one at a time. Each cow wears a transmitter round its neck. When cow number 32 arrives, the system recognises that cow number 32 has arrived. The transmitter acts like a remote control unit for a television, with each cow tuned to its own channel.

    Remote control ICs and infra red sources and sensors are comparatively inexpensive. RS Components do information sheets on theirs.

Development work before you submit your title and specifications

Before submitting this as an examination project, make sure that you can make a working system from your flowchart. If you want to use a computer, translate it into a computer program. Alternatively, work out a block diagram for a non-computerised system.

PROJECT 11

Quiz game controller for public use

This project requires knowledge of most of the Information bank.

The problem

In some games a number of teams or individuals, usually two or four, compete to be first to answer a question. The contestants get the chance to answer by being the first to press the button. Their light comes on and there may be an audible signal. The control system should prevent the other competitors from activating the system, and it should provide a time-up signal if the referee has not reset the system in the allotted answering time.

If the system is to be usable for a public competition, LEDs just will not do, and for maximum dramatic effect any audible signal should be something other than a little buzz.

Further points to consider before writing your specifications

1 **Lights**   What minimum power would be adequate? If you want to use mains voltage lights, study the safety precautions in Project 9. Would lights which require a car battery voltage be acceptable?

2 **Audible signals**   If your sound output transducer used the same power source as the lights, the control system could be battery-operated. Could this affect the pattern of sound that you should try to produce?

3 Four separate contestants' switches, a referee's switch and control box, four lights, a sound output unit and a high-power source could mean a jumble of loose wires. How will you organise the system so that it is easy to set up for use, easy to transport and never ends up as a mess of tangled wires?

Preparing the specifications

Begin by listing, in detail and in the correct order, exactly what the system must do.

Add your decisions about lights, sound output and presentation of the system. Be as precise as you reasonably can be, but try to avoid stating a requirement that you may later want to modify.

Developing the prototype

Follow the instructions on p. 5.

You may find it useful if you first work out a suitable block diagram for Project 6. However, you will then discover that the simplest solution for Project 6 is not easily extendable to more than two contestants.

You should then consider the use of this arrangement in your system.

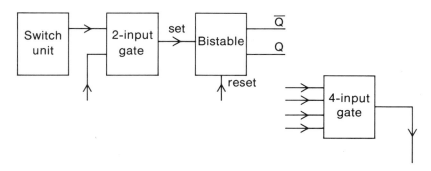

Details of four-input gates can be found in the *CMOS Cookbook*.

Child alarm

This project requires knowledge of most of the Information bank. (It can be undertaken by a small group of people investigating different detection systems or different parts of the system.)

The problem

If a baby or a small child crawls or walks through a doorway, an alarm should sound. An older child or an adult should be able to walk through the doorway without triggering the alarm.

The solution seems to be fairly straightforward: have two beams (of light, or infra red, or ultrasound) across the doorway. The alarm should sound if the lower beam is broken and the upper beam is not broken.

You will find it useful at this point to draw a block diagram of the system described so far. Keep your options open as regards type of beam, and remember that once the alarm is triggered it should remain on.

The first complication

People walking are different from cartons on a conveyor belt. A person's torso reaches the doorway slightly later than the first leg.

Work out how to cope with this complication. You need a new block diagram.

Preparing the specifications

You are now in a position to write your detailed pre-production specifications. Item 1 will be a statement of the basic requirement. After that you must list your decisions regarding:
- your proposed solution to the walking problem,
- the precise sound pattern that you want the alarm to produce,
- the power supply to the system.

Include sketches showing what the various parts of the boxed system might look like and how they might have to be arranged for optimum performance.

The second complication

Optical and infra red systems which use cheap sources and sensors coupled to simple circuitry work very well over very short distances. It is more difficult to use them across something as wide as a doorway. An ultrasonic transmitter and receiver will work well over a much greater range but the transducers cost more, the simplest circuitry is more complicated and it is harder to produce adequately focussed beams.

Making this part of your system work reliably is likely to be your biggest headache. There follows some information which might be useful to you. It is mostly taken from the data sheets of RS components.

Ultrasonic transmitter and receiver

The following circuits show how the transducers may be used in remote control applications. Either of the transmitter circuits may be used with the receiver. The frequency of oscillation is adjusted by means of VR1 for maximum sensitivity. The CMOS circuit allows direct interfacing with logic circuitry. In the receiver VR2 is adjusted for maximum sensitivity.

Note   The relay energises when a signal is received from the transmitter.

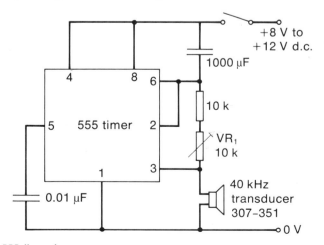

Transmitter using 555 timer i.c.

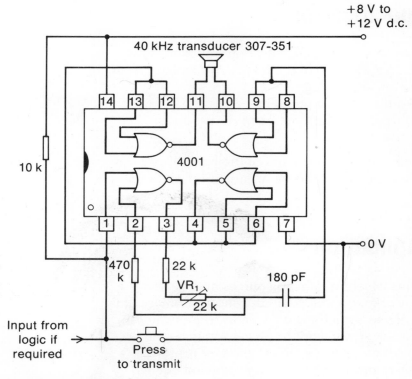

Transmitter using CMOS gate IC 4001B

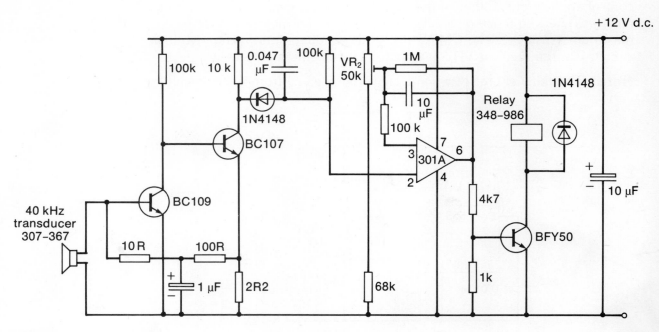

Receiver

Light-dependent resistor ORP12

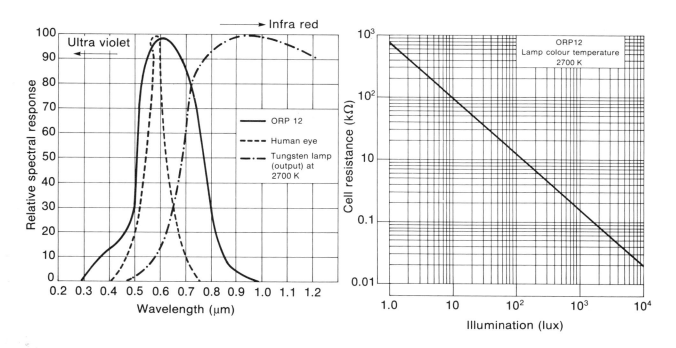

Guide to source illuminations

Light source	Illumination (lux)
Moonlight	0.1
60 W bulb at 1 m	50
1 W MES bulb at 0.1 m	100
Fluorescent lighting	500
Bright sunlight	30 000

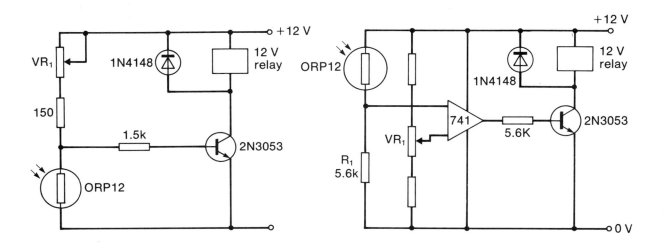

Light emitting diodes

	Intensity of radiation	Wavelength at which intensity is greatest	Rated current	Voltage drop across the diode
Standard red LED	5 mcd	635 nm	10 mA	2 V
Ultrabright red LED	125 mcd	635 nm	20 mA	2.2 V
Superbright (Rapid Electronics)	250 mcd	650 nm	20 mA	1.7 V

General purpose photodiode

When the diode is reverse biased there is a tiny current which increases linearly with illumination. To detect the cutting of a light beam you could use it with a resistor just as you would use an LDR.

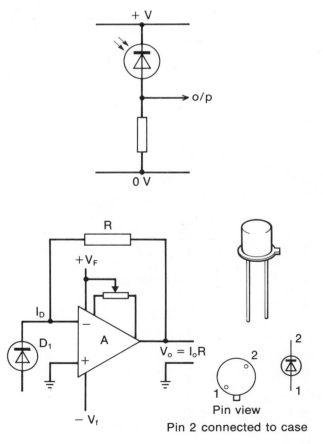

Technical specification

Peak spectral response	750 nm
Change in leakage current (with incident light)	0.7 μA/mW/cm^3 (typ.)
Dark current (at −20 V)	1.4 nA (typ.)
Temp. coeff. of dark current	×2 for 10 °C temp. rise
Reverse breakdown voltage	−80 V at 10 μA
Temp. coeff. of change in leakage current with illumination	0.35%/ °C
Max. forward current	100 mA
Max. dissipation	200 mW at 25 °C
Capacitance (−10 V bias)	12 pF
Response time	250 ns typ.

A general purpose photodiode mounted in a TO18-style case with end window. When reverse biased the leakage current increases proportionately to the incident light. Suitable for use in photometers, modulated light detectors or high-speed counting in punched card tape readers, etc.

Pin view

Pin 2 connected to case

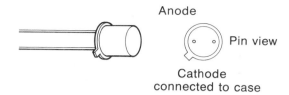

Anode

Pin view

Cathode
connected to case

A planar 1 mm² silicon PIN photodiode housed in a TO18-style case hermetically sealed with an integral plain glass window. The cathode is electrically connected to the case. The device features low junction capacitance, short switching times and, because of its high frequency response, is capable of detecting wide bandwidth signals.

Applications include alarm systems, shaft encoders, light fluctuation and high speed pulse detection.

Technical specification

Peak spectral response	850 nm
Responsivity at 850 nm	0.55 A/W
Rise time of photo current	
t_r (R_L=50 Ω, V_R=20 V, λ=900 nm)	0.5 ns typ., 1 ns max
Capacitance (V_R=0 V	15 pF
(V_R=1 V)	12 pF
(V_R=20 V)	3.5 pF
Cut-off frequency	
(R_L=50 Ω, V_R=20 V, λ=900 nm)	500 MHz
Dark current (V_R=20 V, E=0)	1 nA typ., 5 nA max.
Noise equivalent power (V_R=20 V)	3.3×10^{14} W/$\sqrt{\text{Hz}}$
Power dissipation, max.	250 mW
Breakdown voltage	50 V

Data sheet 2135 December 81 available.

High power infra red source and sensor

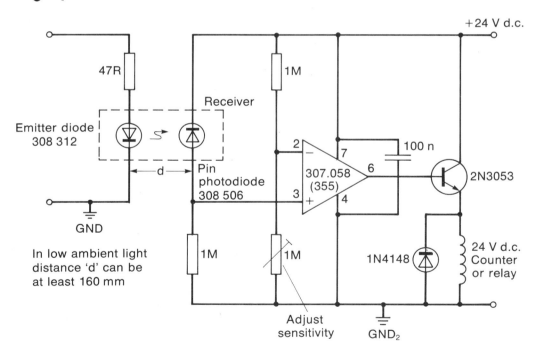

In low ambient light distance 'd' can be at least 160 mm

Note With no illumination from the emitter adjust the IM trimmer, whilst the receiver is in ambient light, until the relay energises. Then reverse adjustment until the relay just de-energises. This compensates for the ambient light level.

Information bank

1 Arranging building blocks to do useful jobs

System A

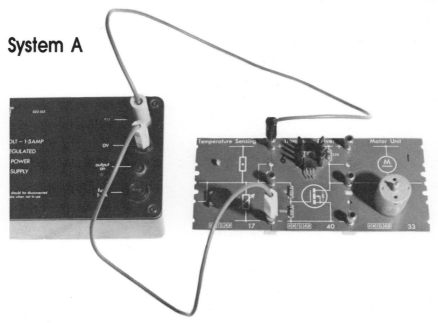

The photograph shows a complete *electronic system* made from a kit of parts. Each part is called a **module**, or **unit**. The structure of the system can be represented by a **block diagram**.

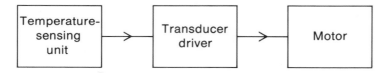

The arrows show that the temperature-sensing unit controls the transducer driver which in turn controls the motor (the direction of flow of information).

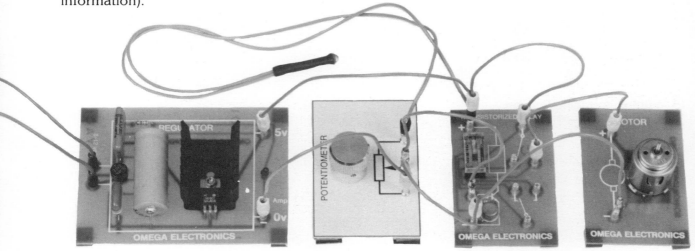

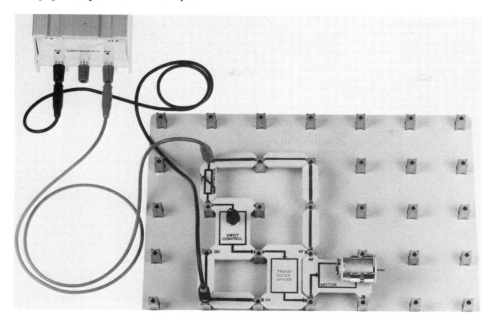

This photograph and those on p. 64 show how different kits can be used to make the same system.

What the system does
If the temperature-sensing unit is hot enough, the motor is on. If the temperature-sensing unit is cold, the motor is off.

How it could be used
The motor could operate a desk fan. The fan would turn on if the air in the room became too hot.

System B

For System B the block diagram looks like this.

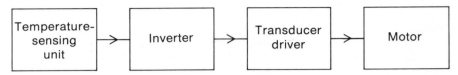

What the system does
If the temperature-sensing unit is hot, the motor is off. If the temperature-sensing unit is cold, the motor is on.

How it could be used
The motor could operate a fan in a hot air central heating system. If the air in a room became too cold, the fan would turn on and hot air would be forced into the room.

System C

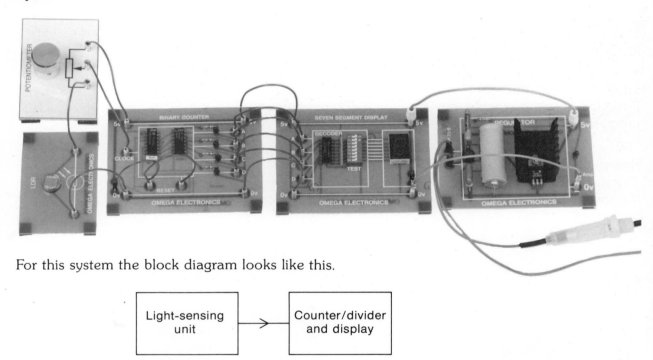

For this system the block diagram looks like this.

No transducer driver is needed for a counter/divider and display

What the system does
If you start with the light-sensing unit in darkness and then switch a light on, the count increases by one. If you then turn the light off the count does not change.

How it could be used
The light-sensing unit could be to one side of a conveyor belt with a lamp at the other side of the belt. The system would count the number of cans or cartons that passed along the conveyor.

System D

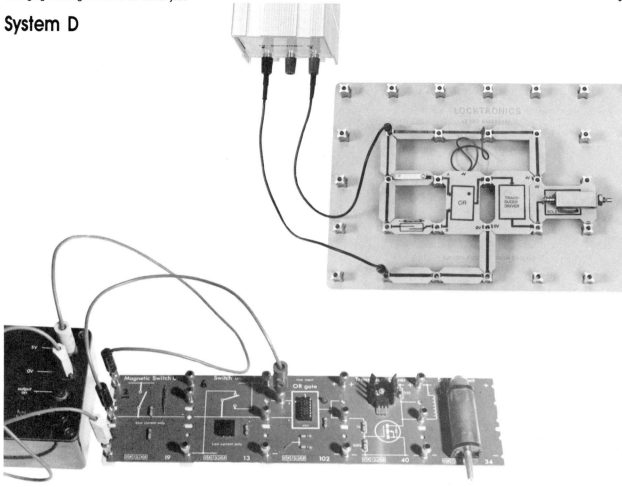

For this system the block diagram looks like this.

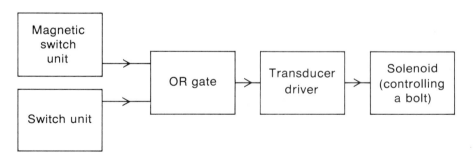

What the system does

The bolt is pulled into the solenoid if a magnet comes close to the magnetic switch unit OR if the button on the ordinary switch unit is pressed.

How it could be used

The solenoid could be fixed to a door. The bolt which the solenoid pulls could be the door bolt. The magnetic switch unit could be activated by a plastic card with a strip of magnetic tape on it that fits into a slot cut into the outside of the door. The ordinary switch could be on the inside of the door.

Building and testing systems

Select a system shown on this page. Build it, find out
what it does, then try to work out a use for it.
Record your work under the headings shown here.

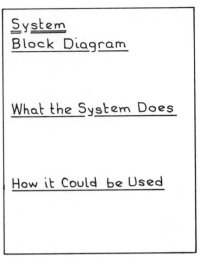

System E

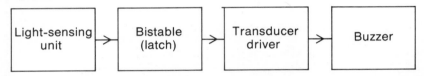

System F

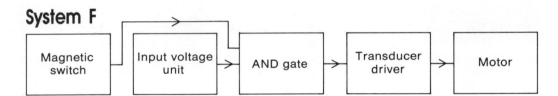

System G

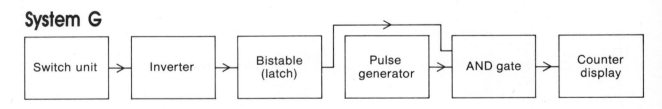

System H

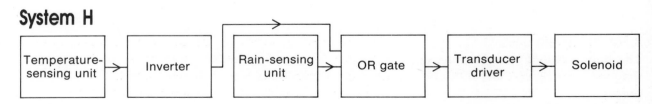

System I

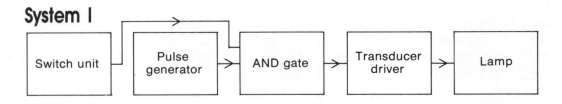

Information which may be useful when designing systems

Arrows on block diagrams show what is controlling what.

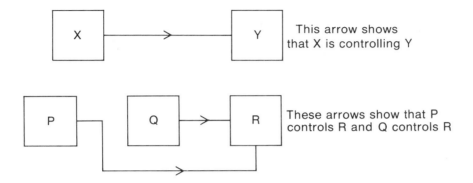

This arrow shows that X is controlling Y

These arrows show that P controls R and Q controls R

Units always fit together according to the following basic pattern.

The **input unit**, i.e. the unit which receives information from outside the electronic system.	**Processing units** which allow the input units to control the output units in different ways.	**Transducer driver**, which ensures that there is enough power to drive the output unit.	The **output unit**, i.e. the device which the electronic system has to control.
input voltage unit light-sensing unit temperature-sensing unit rain-sensing unit switch unit magnetic switch unit (and pulse generator)	invertor (NOT gate) AND gate OR gate bistable (latch)		bulb buzzer motor solenoid counter and display

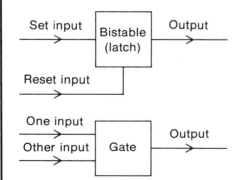

The bistable is turned on by an electrical signal at its set input. Once the bistable is on it stays on. It can only be turned off by a signal at its reset input. The reset signal could be obtained from another unit or by pressing the reset button. Some manufacturers call the bistable unit a **latch**.

If you want the operation of an output unit to depend upon two things, you must use a gate.

Systems which require gates

We may want an output device to be on only if the light level is high enough AND a switch is pressed. An AND gate is needed to enable the two input units to control the output.

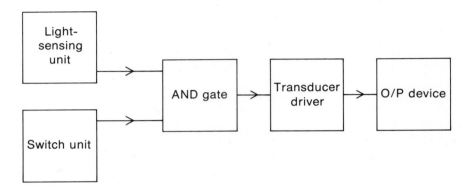

If we want the output device to turn on if the light level is **low** enough AND a switch is pressed, we use a NOT gate as well as an AND gate.

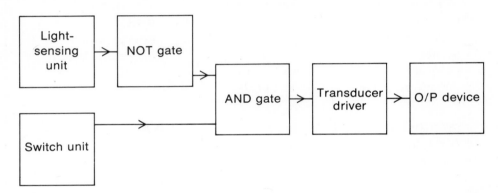

It works because 'light level low' is like saying 'light level NOT high'. The NOT gate inverts the action of the light-sensing unit. An **inverter** is another name for a NOT gate.

Use the modules listed here to produce systems which work as described on the opposite page.

input voltage unit	AND gate	transducer	various o/p
light-sensing unit	OR gate	driver	devices
magnetic switch unit	NOT gate (inverter)		motor,
rain-sensing unit			solenoid,
switch unit			bulb,
temperature-sensing unit			buzzer

Always draw your idea as a block diagram before trying it out, and always start the drawing by putting your chosen input units on the left.

An output device should be on only if:

(a) it is not raining,

(b) it is dark,

(c) it is raining at night,

(d) it is not cold and the humidity is high,

(e) it is cold or dark,

(f) two light beams are cut or a switch is pressed,

(g) a light beam is cut and either a magnet is in position or a switch is pressed,

(h) the soil is dry and the plant height indicator shows that the plant is wilting. (For plant height indication consider using an input voltage unit with a long lever to turn the knob.)

Working it out without apparatus

Say what these systems do.

System J

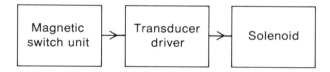

System K

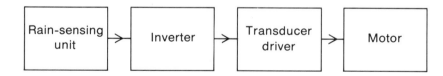

System L

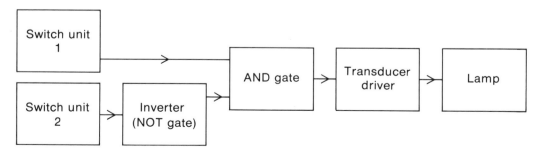

System M

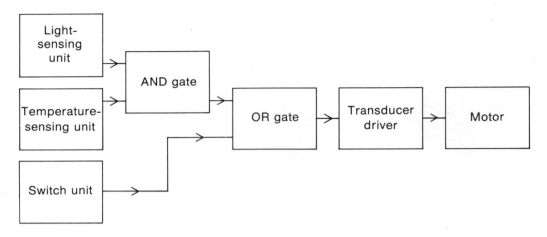

System N

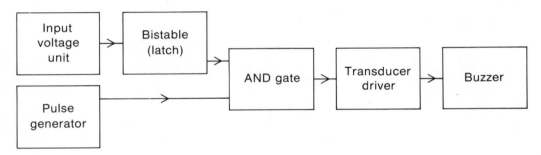

Designing your own systems

For each of the following problems work out a system which might be appropriate and present your ideas by drawing a block diagram and describing what your system does.

Problem O   Some people tend to 'borrow' things when you are not watching. It could be useful if an alarm sounded whenever someone moved your pencil case.

Problem P   A locust cage needs to be warmed slightly during the daytime. A simple way is to provide a lamp which automatically turns on in the day and off at night.

Problem Q   Clothes drying on a line sometimes get wet because of a sudden shower. It could be useful if a warning sound was produced as soon as it started to rain.

Problem R   A flashing lamp attracts your attention more effectively than a lamp which is on continuously. Can you arrange for a lamp to be flashing but only when a baby has wet its bed?

Hint: The lamp is controlled by wetness **and** by something else.

Problem S   A solenoid which is continually switched on and off can make a bolt (or something like it) move backwards and forwards continually. Could you help the producer of a play who needs a tapping sound to be produced automatically whenever an actor stands in a chosen place?

Problem T   Imagine that you have a switch unit with an extremely sensitive switch that closes when you blow gently on it. (Such switches are obtainable.) A limbless person or a patient who is bedridden and immobilised cannot easily call a nurse. Could you devise a system so that a brief blow down a tube triggers a bleeping alarm that continues to bleep until the nurse resets it?

2 Microprocessors in use

Chips that can be programmed

A **silicon chip** is a tiny slice of an element called silicon into which an electronic circuit has been built. It is only about 1 mm square. This is too small to handle, so it is enclosed in plastic with gold wires connecting it to pins. The complete package is called an **integrated circuit** (or **IC** for short).

A single IC controls the movement of information in all parts of a computer. The same IC does all the calculations and takes all the decisions. An IC that does all this is called a **microprocessor**.

A microprocessor

A microprocessor is a very special sort of electronic circuit because it can be **programmed**. This means that you can alter what it does without changing the circuit. You simply have to give it new instructions.

> A microprocessor is used when you want to choose different sequences of actions. An ordinary electronic circuit is extremely complicated if it has to cope with even a few different sequences.

The control panel of a video recorder

You can program the microprocessor in a video recorder to perform a complicated sequence of actions. You just have to press a few switches. For example:

8.00	switch on channel 3
8.30	switch off channel 3
10.45	switch on channel 2
11.45	switch off channel 2
	. . . and so on.

Obviously you can choose a different sequence every day.

Automatic washing machines

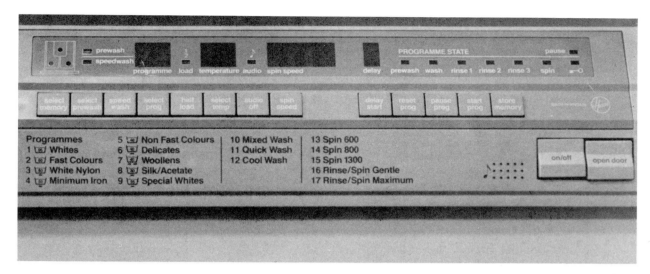

The control panel of the Hoover A3492 Computer Control 1300 washing machine

The **fast colours** program is used for cotton and linen articles which are colourfast at 60 °C. The program starts like this.

1 Open the pre-wash valve to allow water to come in.

2 After 5 seconds, open the main-wash valve as well.

3 When the water has reached the required level, close both valves.

4 Raise the water temperature to 50 °C and turn the drum at normal washing speed (52 revolutions per minute).
   (a) For 6 minutes the drum repeatedly turns for 15 seconds and stops for 5 seconds.
   (b) For 10 minutes the drum turns for 5 seconds and stops for 15 seconds.
   (c) For 5 minutes the drum turns for 15 seconds and stops for 5 seconds.

There is yet more to the main wash sequence. This is followed by three different rinse sequences, then three different spin sequences.

Obviously a washing machine uses a complicated sequence of actions. Also you can select from many different sequences. All of these sequences are programmed into the microprocessor at the time it is manufactured. This makes it very easy for the user to select a complete sequence of operations.

In less advanced washing machines, all of this had to be controlled by a very complicated set of cog wheels and switches. People expect the microprocessor systems to work reliably for longer than the old mechanical controllers. Also it is easier to make them control a wider range of more complicated wash routines.

Microwave ovens

The microprocessor in the Electrolux 4076 oven allows you to program a complicated sequence of actions. The combination of ten number keys and eight function keys also allows you to program a wide variety of different sequences.

The instruction book uses examples to teach you how to program the oven. Each example uses a column of boxes to show you what to do. Some examples of these instructions are given here. Other types of program include delayed start, defrosting, browning, and cooking to a selected temperature.

The control panel of the Electrolux Mealmaker microwave oven, model 4076

Setting the cook programmes

Example 1
Basic one-step cooking at HIGH (100%) power level
Setting the oven to cook at **high** (100%), for any specified length of time, is the easiest programme because the oven automatically cooks at the **high** power level, unless you programme it for a lower power level.

Normally you would first touch 'Programme 1'. However, since 'Programme 1' is the most common use, you may skip the 'Programme 1' pad . . . the control will assume this is what you want.

As an example:

Power level: HIGH (100%)
Total cooking time: 45 seconds

Step 1

First, I push the ON button

Step 2

I want to cook for 45 seconds on High (100%) → 4

Touch '4' then '5' (don't touch 'POWER SELECTOR' because High (100%) is automatic) → 5

Step 3

I'm ready to start cooking → START

Touch 'START'

That's all there is to it and 45 seconds later it will stop. Four short bleeps later it will tell me that the cooking is finished

Example 2
Learning to set a different power

Here's an example that specifies cooking at **medium-high** (70%) instead of the **high** (100%) power level:

Power level: MEDIUM-HIGH (70%)
Total cooking time: 20 minutes

Step 1

First, I push the ON button

Step 2

I want to cook for 20 minutes | 2

Touch '2' then '0' three times | 0

| 0 |

You always have to include the number of seconds after the minutes | 0 |

Step 3

I want to use Medium/high (70%) | POWER SELECTOR

Touch 'POWER SELECTOR' then '7' | 7

Step 4

I am ready to start cooking | START

Touch 'START'

Twenty minutes later the oven will stop and signal. I can test for 'doneness' and cook a few minutes more if needed

Example 3
Using the 'Programme 2' pad to set two different power levels in one cooking programme

Microwave recipes sometimes call for food to be cooked at one power level for a length of time, then at a different power level for another period of time. You can programme the oven to do this automatically.

Here's an example:

Power level:
  HIGH (100%) for 8 minutes and
  MEDIUM (50%) for 70 minutes
Total cooking time:
  1 hour, 18 minutes

Step 1

push the ON button

Step 2

First cook for 8 minutes | PROGRAM ONE

Touch 'PROGRAM ONE' then '8' then '0' twice | 8

Step 3

Cook at High (100%) for this period | 0

High is automatic, no need to touch anything | 0

Step 4

Then cook for 1 hour 10 min more | PROGRAM TWO

Touch 'PROGRAM TWO' then '7' then '0' three times (1 hour 10 min is 70 min) | 7

| 0 |
| 0 |
| 0 |

Step 5

Cook at Medium (50%) for this period | POWER SELECTOR

Touch 'POWER SELECTOR' then '5' | 5

Step 6

Ready to start | START

Touch 'START'

The Jaguar XJ40

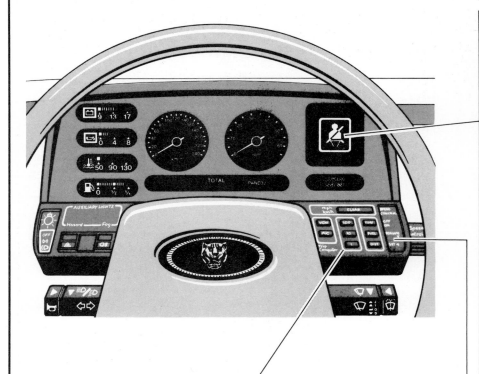

The condition of the car is monitored continuously by many sensors. If a fault is found, the **vehicle condition monitor** displays the fault.

BRAKE FAILURE — LOW BRAKE PRESSURE — FASTEN SEAT BELT — DOOR OPEN

BRAKE PAD LOW — BRAKE FLUID LOW

WASHER FLUID LOW — FUELLING FAILURE

COOLANT LEVEL LOW — BULB FAILURE

The trip computer uses data from one of the microprocessors continuously. It can be programmed by push-buttons to display average and instantaneous fuel consumption, the amount of fuel used on the journey, the range, the distance travelled, the distance to go, the average speed, the time the journey has taken, and the time the journey will take.

Seven microprocessors are used to control all key systems in the XJ40

The Jaguar XJ40

The microprocessor-based cruise control system will maintain a previously selected speed without the driver ever having to use the throttle or the brake. On a long motorway journey, the driver will only have to use the throttle or brake in an emergency. The main sensor used in this system is a speed sensor.

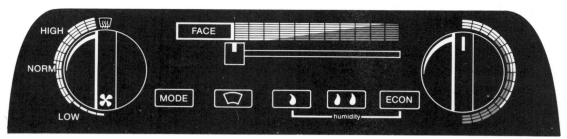

The environment
control panel

The **air-conditioning system** controls the conditions inside the car
according to the comfort levels selected by the driver.

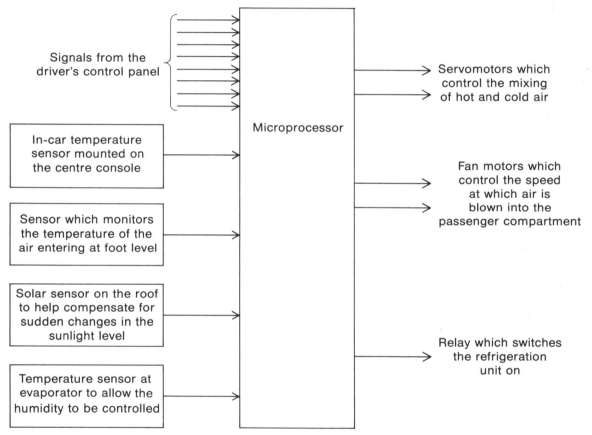

**The main inputs to, and outputs from, the air-conditioning system's microprocessor.
The temperature sensors are temperature-sensitive transistors; they generate a voltage which is
proportional to the absolute temperature.**

Once the driver has selected the required air temperature for inside the
car, that temperature will be maintained in all weather conditions.

A face-level air temperature control allows the driver to select a different
temperature for air which enters through the fascia panel vents. This can
be up to 30 °C cooler than foot-level air.

The system can be set to take different amounts of moisture from the
incoming air, so that the humidity can be controlled independently of the
temperature.

Sensors

Most microprocessor systems need an input of information from **sensors**.
Sensors convert non-electronic information into a form which can be used
by electronic circuits. For example:

- a **light sensor** produces electrical changes which follow changes of
  light level,

- a **temperature sensor** produces electrical changes which follow
  changes of temperature,

- a **pressure sensor** produces electrical changes which follow changes of
  pressure,

- a **water level sensor** produces an electrical change when water
  reaches a set level.

Questions

3.6 litre Engine management system

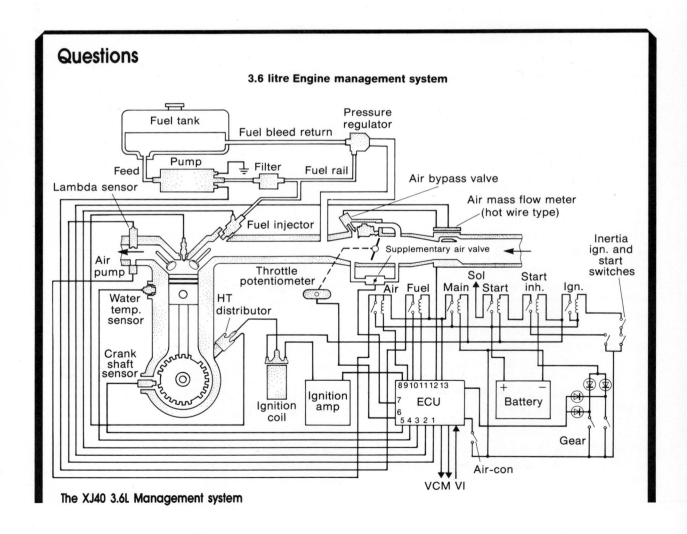

The XJ40 3.6L Management system

1 The Jaguar's engine management system has to ensure maximum power for minimum fuel consumption.
A number of sensors are used to feed information into the microprocessor which is part of the engine control unit (ECU).

(a) One of the sensors is a resistor whose resistance decreases with increasing temperature.
Work out which one this is.

(b) One of the sensors monitors the exhaust gases to check that they satisfy national standards relating to pollution of the atmosphere.
Work out from its position which one does this job.

(c) Two sensors are shown which do not have the word 'sensor' in their name. Study the diagram and pick them out. (If you need help, one of them is described on p. 147.)

(d) Some of the connections to the ECU have been numbered. Write out the numbers of the five which carry information **into** the ECU.

2 (a) List all of the sensors that are mentioned on pp. 78 and 79.

(b) Which type of program in a microwave oven would use information from a sensor?
What sensor will it use?

(c) What sensors do you think feed information into a washing machine's microprocessor?

(d) What sensor (if any) feeds information into a video recorder's microprocessor?

3 Study the three microwave oven programs.
Draw columns of boxes to show what is needed for the following operations:

(a) to heat a mug of milk for $1\frac{1}{2}$ minutes at full power,

(b) to cook some scrambled egg for 2 minutes at 80% power,

(c) to cook a meringue for 3 minutes at 50% power, then for 5 minutes at full power.

4 A toy car has to follow the route shown in the drawing. The car has three wheels. Each rear wheel is driven by its own motor.

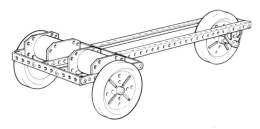

The toy car

When a motor is on, the wheel moves forward 80 mm in one second.
In the diagram most dots show distances of 80 mm. You will have to work out the distances for the 45° angles.

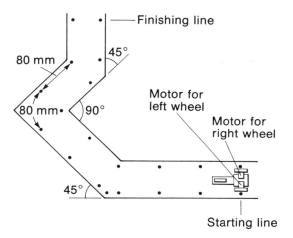

The route

Draw a column of boxes to show when the motors have to be on.
Begin like this:

> Both motors on
> for 3 seconds

5 An ordinary electronic circuit could be designed to carry out the motor control program of question 4.
No microprocessor would be needed.

(a) What would be the advantage of using a microprocessor system to control the car?

(b) What sensors would be needed?

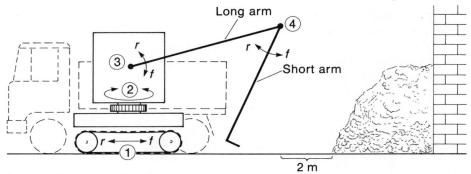

Long arm

Short arm

2 m

6 The diagram shows an idea for a robot dumper. A lorry waits on the far side of the dumper. The pile of rubbish must be loaded on to the lorry.

The main sections of the dumper are controlled by four motors which you have to program.

Draw a column of boxes to show how to lift one shovelful of rubbish onto the lorry and get the shovel back into position for the next load.

Some possible ways to begin are:

Motor 1 forward until shovel reaches rubbish	**OR**	Motor 1 forward 2 metres	**OR**	Motor 4 forward until short arm vertical

7 A lift operates between two floors. A passenger entering the lift must press a button to operate the mechanism.

The door has to close safely. It must not injure anyone who may be in the doorway.

On reaching the other level, the door must open and close automatically.

Copy the flowchart and complete it using the statements. Some statements will be needed more than once.

Statements
- Door closes slowly
- Door opens quickly
- Fixed time delay
- Is there resistance to door closing?
- Door closed, lift moves to other floor

A set of statement boxes linked by arrows is called a **flowchart**. We use flowcharts because they help us to solve problems which have sequences of actions.

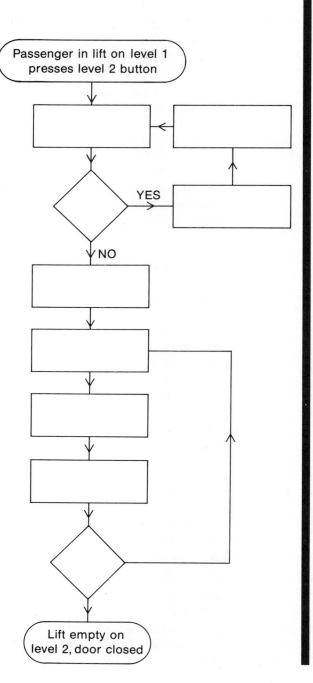

Passenger in lift on level 1 presses level 2 button

YES

NO

Lift empty on level 2, door closed

8 **(a)** Explain why a microprocessor is **not** likely to be used to control the lift in question 7.

  (b) How could resistance to the door closing be detected?

9 A farmer needs a system to feed the hens automatically. A fixed amount of food should be transferred from the main food bin to the feeding trough once every four hours. If the trough is more than a quarter full, food should not be transferred to it.

Draw a flowchart to show how the system operates. You only need three statements:

● Is the trough more than $\frac{1}{4}$ full?
● Transfer food
● Wait 4 hours

10 Why do you think microprocessors **are** used in automatic hen feeding systems?

3 Control from a computer keyboard

Make sure that you understand binary counting (see p. 139) before studying this chapter.

Information in a computer

If you press any key on a computer keyboard, a binary number is produced inside the computer. If you type, 'My project is a disaster', the computer stores it as a set of binary numbers. All information in a computer is stored as sets of binary numbers.

Imagine a computer drawing a picture on the screen. Inside the computer, binary numbers are moving from place to place and changing to different values.

A computer has to store many thousands of binary numbers. Each individual store is called a **register**. A register is like a box with eight compartments. It can hold only one 8-bit number at a time.

Ø	Ø	Ø	Ø	1	1	1	Ø	1

A register holding the number thirteen

Each register has its own address. The address is just a number with no street name or place name.

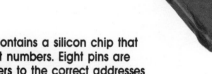

This 24-pin IC package contains a silicon chip that can store 16 384 eight-bit numbers. Eight pins are used to guide the numbers to the correct addresses

On a BBC computer, if you type (in BASIC)

`?65121 = 13` `RETURN`

you will send the number thirteen to the register whose address is **65121**.

If you type

`?647Ø5 = 13` `RETURN`

you will send the number thirteen to address **64705**.

The 1 MHz bus, user port and printer port under the BBC Master computer

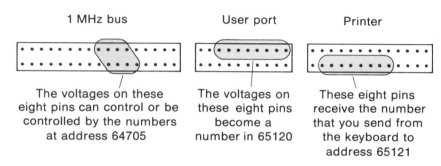

1 MHz bus	User port	Printer

The voltages on these eight pins can control or be controlled by the numbers at address 64705

The voltages on these eight pins become a number in 65120

These eight pins receive the number that you send from the keyboard to address 65121

Three of the ports that are under a BBC computer

Controlling the printer port

Eight pins at the printer port receive the number at address **65121**.

If you type

`?65121 = Ø` RETURN

all eight pins will be at low voltage (0 V).

If you type

`?65121 = 255` RETURN

all pins will be at high voltage (5 V).

If you type

`?65121 = 13` RETURN

three pins will be at 5 V and the others will be at 0 V. The three pins at 5 V represent the 1's in the 8-bit number 0 0 0 0 1 1 0 1.

You can use the keyboard to control the voltages at the individual pins, so now you can control the world!

Controlling the 1 MHz bus

Eight pins at the 1 MHz bus connector receive the number at address **64705**.

If you type

`?64705 = Ø` RETURN

all eight pins will be at low voltage (0 V).

If you type

`?64705 = 255` RETURN

all eight pins will be at high voltage (5 V).

If you type

`?64705 = 13` RETURN

three pins will be at 5 V and the others will be at 0 V. The three pins at 5 V represent the 1's in the 8-bit number 0 0 0 0 1 1 0 1.

Getting information into and out of a computer

Between the computer and the outside world you need something which:

- can control extra power to drive motors and solenoids,
- can pass electrical signals from other apparatus into the computer,
- is easy to make connections to.

It is called a **buffer box** or **interface**.

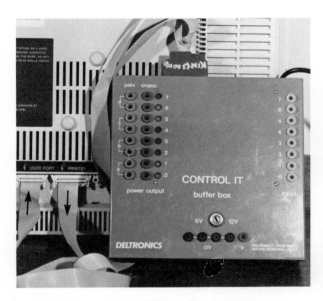

The Deltronics buffer box. The arrows show that information flows from the CONTROL IT buffer box to the user port. Other information flows from the printer port to the buffer box

The INTERPACK 2 buffer box. The arrows show that information can flow either way along the ribbon cable that connects INTERPACK 2 with the 1 MHz bus

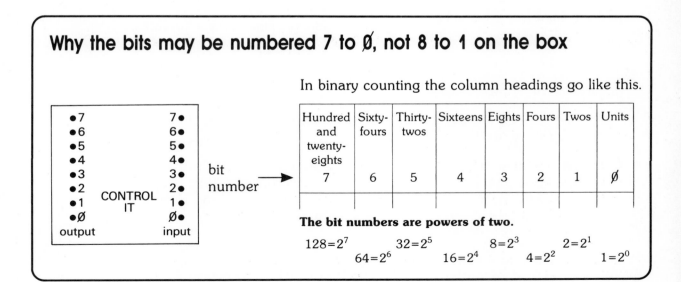

Why the bits may be numbered 7 to Ø, not 8 to 1 on the box

In binary counting the column headings go like this.

Hundred and twenty-eights	Sixty-fours	Thirty-twos	Sixteens	Eights	Fours	Twos	Units
7	6	5	4	3	2	1	Ø

The bit numbers are powers of two.

$$128 = 2^7 \qquad 32 = 2^5 \qquad 8 = 2^3 \qquad 2 = 2^1$$
$$64 = 2^6 \qquad 16 = 2^4 \qquad 4 = 2^2 \qquad 1 = 2^0$$

```
  •7        7•
  •6        6•
  •5        5•
  •4        4•
  •3        3•
  •2        2•
  •1  CONTROL  1•
  •Ø    IT   Ø•
 output     input
```

bit number →

Programming for control of the printer port and the 1 MHz bus

> **Note** Instead of outport address you type **65121** or **6470 5**, depending upon which port you are using.

Program 1A

```
1Ø  ? outport address = 15          ← LEDs show 8+4+2+1.
2Ø  TIME=Ø :  REPEAT UNTIL  TIME=2ØØ  ← They stay on for two seconds
3Ø  ? outport address = 6Ø          ← LEDs  show  32+16+8+4.
4Ø  TIME=Ø :  REPEAT UNTIL  TIME=4ØØ  ← They stay on for four seconds.
5Ø  ? outport address = Ø           ← All LEDs off.
```

If you enter and **RUN** the program, the LEDs will show what is happening[†].

TIME = Ø resets the computer's internal counter to zero.

REPEAT UNTIL TIME = 2ØØ allows the counter to count up to 200. This takes two seconds because **the counter takes 1 second to count up to 100**.

Line 2Ø of program 1 therefore causes a 2 second delay before the computer moves to line 3Ø.

Line 4Ø of program 1 causes a 4 second delay before the computer moves to line 5Ø.

Program 1B (continuous recycling of 1A)

Enter the following program. It is the same as program 1A except for line 5Ø.

```
1Ø  ? outport address =  15
2Ø  TIME=Ø :  REPEAT UNTIL  TIME=2ØØ
3Ø  ? outport address =  6Ø
4Ø  TIME=Ø :  REPEAT UNTIL  TIME=4ØØ
5Ø  GOTO 1Ø  ← means 'go back to line 1Ø and do it all again'.
```

RUN the program. When you want to stop it, press ESCAPE.

[†]Some interface units do not have LEDs. A display can be built very simply on prototype board. Information on how to do this and on other interface units is given on p. 196

> Equivalent instructions for RML, ZX Spectrum and IBM machines
> are on pp. 14–17.

Programs 1A and 1B are acceptable for very simple control sequences.
When you require a sequence with more than two steps, use program
2A or 2B.

Program 2A

It is possible to put all of the output information into a single line, called
the DATA line. You can then produce different output patterns just by
altering the DATA line.

```
1Ø  DATA 16,2ØØ,24,2ØØ,Ø,2ØØ,3,1ØØ,1,1ØØ,Ø,Ø
2Ø  READ O,T
3Ø  ?outport address=O———(the letter O, not Ø)
4Ø  IF T=Ø THEN END
5Ø  TIME=Ø : REPEAT UNTIL TIME=T
6Ø  GOTO 2Ø
```

Enter and RUN the program.

The DATA line contains the following sequence:

16,2ØØ	← LEDs show 16 for two seconds.
24,2ØØ	← LEDs show 16 + 8 for two seconds.
Ø,2ØØ	← LEDs show all off for two seconds.
3,1ØØ	← LEDs show 2 + 1 for one second.
1,1ØØ	← LEDs show 1 for one second.
Ø,Ø	← LEDs all off. End of run.

Program 2B (continuous recycling of 2A)

Add the following to 2A:

```
7Ø  RESTORE←—Reinstates the data as if the program had not been run.
8Ø  GOTO 1Ø
```

Also change line 4Ø to:
```
4Ø  IF T=Ø THEN 7Ø
```

RUN the program. When you want to stop it, press ESCAPE.

How program 2A works

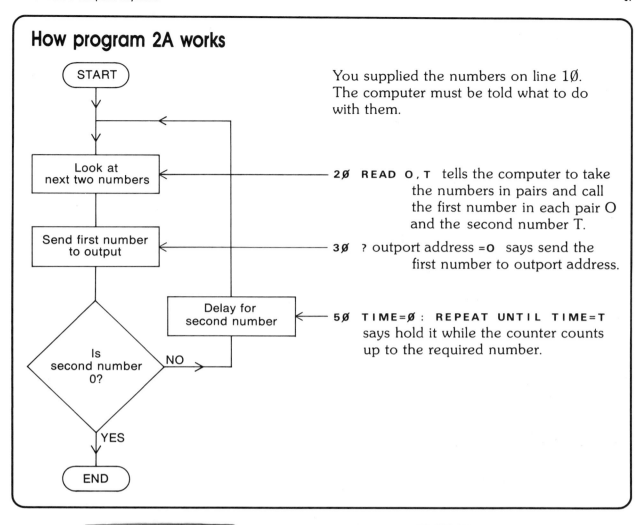

You supplied the numbers on line 1Ø. The computer must be told what to do with them.

2Ø READ O,T tells the computer to take the numbers in pairs and call the first number in each pair O and the second number T.

3Ø ? outport address =O says send the first number to outport address.

5Ø TIME=Ø : REPEAT UNTIL TIME=T says hold it while the counter counts up to the required number.

RML   **IBM**

Equivalent instructions for RML and IBM machines are on pp. 14–17.

Controlling motors (or solenoids or anything else)

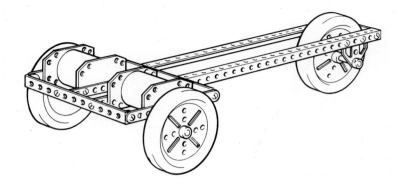

Think of a toy car which has three wheels. Each rear wheel is driven by its own motor. Each motor has to be connected to a different output bit on a buffer box.

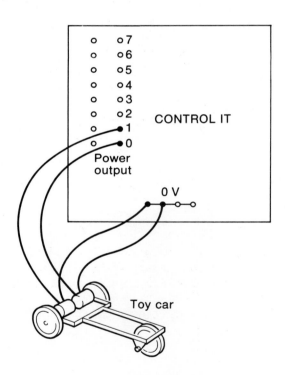

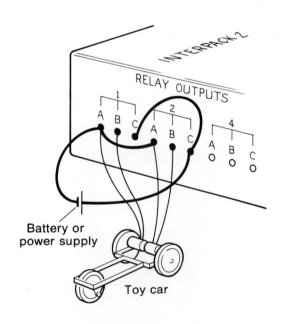

If the buffer box has a full internal power supply, no extra wiring is needed.

?65121=1 turns on one motor
?65121=2 turns on the other motor
?65121=3 turns on both motors

The buffer box cannot provide enough power to drive motors. You need an extra power supply.

?647Ø5=1 turns on one motor
?647Ø5=2 turns on the other motor
?647Ø5=3 turns on both motors

Question 4 on p. 81 required you to work out a sequence for a two-motor car.
You could make it happen now using program **1A** or **2A**.

Questions

1 Convert the following binary numbers into everyday (decimal) form.

    (a) 0 0 0 0 0 0 1 1   **(d)** 1 0 0 0 0 0 1 0
    (b) 1 0 0 0 0 1 0 1   **(e)** 0 0 0 0 1 1 1 1
    (c) 1 1 1 1 0 0 0 0

2 **(a)** What instruction will send the number 22 to address **65121**?
    (b) What instruction will send the number 22 to address **64705**?
    (c) What instruction causes a one second delay before the computer moves to the next instruction?

3 **(a)** What instruction sends the number 254 to address **65121**?
    (b) What instruction sends the number 254 to address **64705**?
    (c) What instruction causes a ten second delay?

4
Step 1: Bit 7 ⊙ ⊙ ⊙ ⊙ ⊙ ☀ ☀ ⊙ Bit 0 for ½ second
Step 2: ⊙ ⊙ ⊙ ⊙ ⊙ ☀ ⊙ ⊙ for ½ second

The light-emitting diodes (LEDs) on a buffer box have to follow the steps shown. The sequence must then recycle continuously.
Write a program to make this happen. Your program could be like program **1B**.

5
Bit 7 ⊙ ⊙ ⊙ ⊙ ⊙ ⊙ ⊙ ⊙ Bit 0 for ← 2 seconds (all off)
⊙ ⊙ ⊙ ⊙ ⊙ ⊙ ☀ ☀ ← for ¼ second
⊙ ⊙ ⊙ ⊙ ☀ ☀ ⊙ ⊙ ← for ¼ second
⊙ ⊙ ⊙ ⊙ ⊙ ☀ ☀ ⊙ ← for ¼ second
⊙ ⊙ ⊙ ☀ ☀ ⊙ ⊙ ⊙ ← for ¼ second

The LEDs on a buffer box have to follow the steps shown. The sequence must then recycle continuously.
Write a program to make this happen. Your program should be like program **2B**.

6 For part of the wash program described on p. 75, the drum has to follow this sequence.

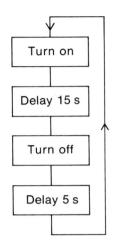

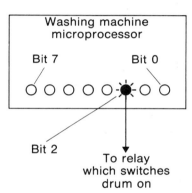

Suppose the drum is controlled by bit 2 of the microprocessor. Write a program to make the drum follow the sequence. Your program could be like program **1B** or program **2B**. (Assume that the outport address = 64.)

In the program described on p. 75, this part lasts for six minutes. During this time it recycles eighteen times. (18 × 20 seconds = 6 minutes.) To make a sequence recycle for a fixed number of times, use a **FOR . . . NEXT** loop:

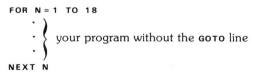

4 Using incoming signals to control a program

In BBC BASIC : PRINT means 'display on the screen'

? means 'the number from (or to)'

Signals arriving at the user port

Using the CONTROL IT box

The voltages at eight pins of the user port become a number at address **65120**.

If you type

PRINT ?6512Ø RETURN

the number 255 appears on the screen.

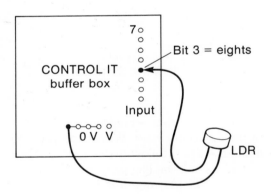

Connect a light-dependent resistor (LDR) to input 3 and one of the 0 V sockets. Allow light to reach the LDR.

Type

PRINT ?6512Ø RETURN

The number 247 appears. (But if the LDR is in darkness 255 appears.)

The number that the computer receives is 255 minus the value of the switched input(s).

Signals arriving at the 1MHz bus

Using INTERPACK 2

On the 1MHz bus connector, the same eight pins can be used to send signals or receive them.†

If you type

PRINT ?647Ø5 RETURN

the number Ø appears on the screen

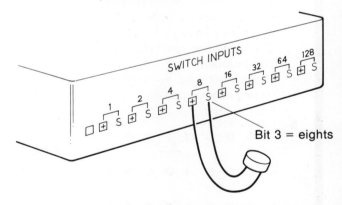

Connect an LDR to the input sockets labelled 8 (i.e. bit 3). Allow light to reach the LDR.

Type

PRINT ?647Ø5 RETURN

The number 8 appears. (But if the LDR is in darkness Ø appears.)

The number that the computer receives is the value of the switched input(s).

†How this works is explained on p. 17.

Equivalent instructions for RML, ZX Spectrum and IBM machines are on pp. 14–17

Programs to make output depend upon input

Connect an LDR to input bit 3, as in the last section.

Using the CONTROL IT box

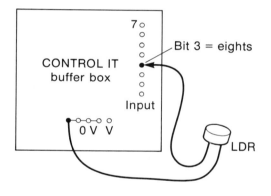

Using INTERPACK 2

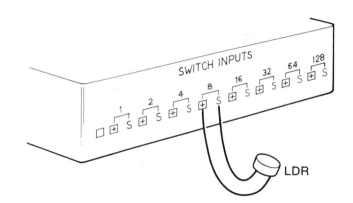

Program 3 (CONTROL IT)

```
1Ø  I=?6512Ø
2Ø  IF I=247 THEN ?65121=4 ELSE
    ?65121=2
3Ø  GOTO 1Ø
```

Program 3 (INTERPACK 2)

```
1Ø  I=?647Ø5
2Ø  IF I=8 THEN ?647Ø5=4 ELSE
    ?647Ø5=2
3Ø  GOTO 1Ø
```

Line 3Ø makes the computer keep on checking the input.

Enter and RUN program **3**. See that:
- with light on the LDR, output LEDs show 4,
- with LDR in darkness, output LEDs show 2.

Try a combination of program 3 with program 1B

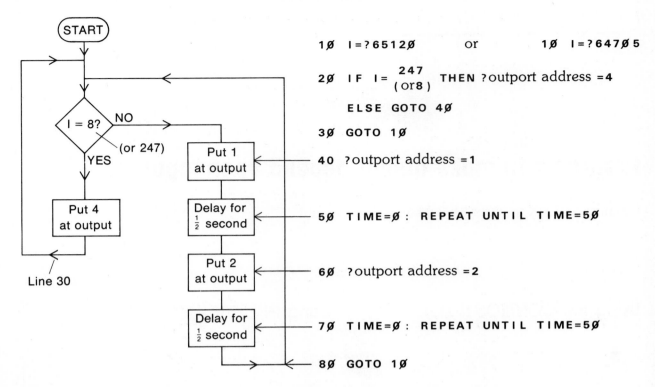

```
1Ø   I=?6512Ø              or              1Ø   I=?647Ø5

2Ø   IF  I=  247       THEN ?outport address =4
            (or8)
     ELSE GOTO 4Ø
3Ø   GOTO 1Ø

40   ?outport address =1

5Ø   TIME=Ø :  REPEAT  UNTIL  TIME=5Ø

6Ø   ?outport address =2

7Ø   TIME=Ø :  REPEAT  UNTIL  TIME=5Ø

8Ø   GOTO 1Ø
```

Program **3** can be combined with program **2B** in a similar fashion.

> Equivalent instructions for RML, ZX Spectrum and IBM machines are on pp. 14–17.

A practical problem

Could you build a structure which would always point towards a light?

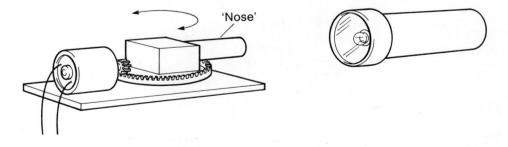

If the torch moves to right or left, the 'nose' should turn with it.

Ideas

1 A simple structure can be made from a kit such as Lego®, Fischertechnik® or Meccano®.

2 The 'nose' could have two LDRs.

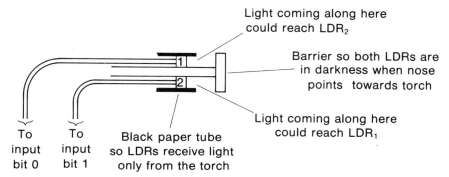

Light coming along here could reach LDR$_2$

Barrier so both LDRs are in darkness when nose points towards torch

Light coming along here could reach LDR$_1$

To input bit 0   To input bit 1   Black paper tube so LDRs receive light only from the torch

3 The motor must be able to turn in both directions.

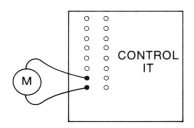 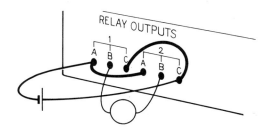

With the connections shown, bit Ø is the on/off control, `?65121=1` turns the motor one way, `?65121=3` turns it the other way.

With the connections shown, `?647Ø5=1` turns the motor one way, `?647Ø5=2` turns it the other way. The operation of this circuit is described on p. 169.

4 Your program has to produce the following behaviour.

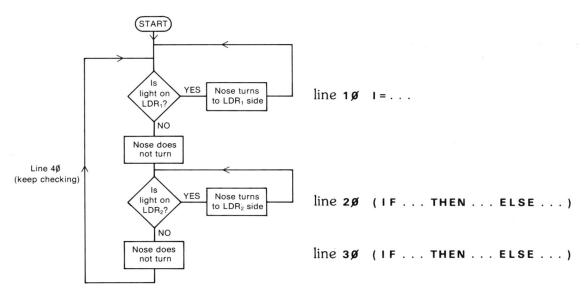

line **1Ø** **I = . . .**

line **2Ø** **(I F . . . THEN . . . ELSE . . .)**

line **3Ø** **(I F . . . THEN . . . ELSE . . .)**

Questions

1

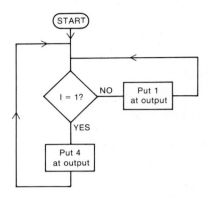

Write a program to make this happen. Your program should be like program **3**.

Write it for the buffer box which you use at your school.

2 The following output behaviour is needed.

Bit 7   Bit 0

○ ○ ○ ○ ○ ○ ☀ ○ ← if an LDR connected to input 0 has light on it

○ ○ ○ ○ ○ ○ ○ ☀ ← if the LDR is in darkness

(a) Draw a flowchart to show this behaviour.
(b) Write a program to make this happen. Your program should be like program **3**. Write it for the buffer box which you use at your school.

3 The following output behaviour is required.

Bit 7   Bit 0

○ ○ ○ ○ ☀ ☀ ○ ○ ← If an LDR connected to input 0 and an LDR connected to input 1 both have light on them

○ ○ ○ ○ ○ ○ ○ ☀ ← If the LDRs do not both have light on them

(a) Draw a flowchart to show this behaviour.
(b) Write a program to make this happen. Your program should be like program **3**.

4 The washing machine program described on p. 75 starts like this:

(1) Open the pre-wash valve.

(2) After 5 seconds, open the main wash valve.

(3) When the water has reached the required level, close both valves.

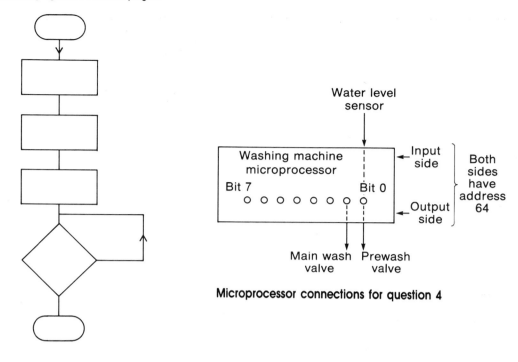

Microprocessor connections for question 4

(a) Copy and complete the flowchart to show the sequence of actions required.

(b) Write a program to make it happen. Assume that the microprocessor has the connections shown in the drawing.

5   This question refers to the practical problem on p. 94.

(a) At the beginning of Chapter 2, a reason was given for using a microprocessor. Does it apply to this problem?

(b) An electronic system to control the motor can be made using two light-sensing units, two transducer drivers and two relays. No microprocessor is needed.
What is the advantage of using computer control first before developing an electronic circuit to do the job?

(c) In many systems where a mechanism is driven by a motor, you need to provide a lot of gearing down to make things go slowly enough.
For this problem is it best for the 'nose' to turn quickly or slowly? Why?

(d) You could use on LDR instead of two, like this:

Long tube of black paper so LDR receives light only when the nose points towards the torch

Try to work out the advantages and disadvantages of using this technique.

Electrical height

How to read a testmeter

The instrument below is called a **testmeter** or **multimeter**. It can be used to measure voltage or current or resistance, depending upon the position of the range selector switch. In the illustration the 10 volts DC range has been selected. The best scale to use with this range is the one that goes 0, 2, 4, 6, 8, 10. The pointer indicates 5.0 volts (usually written 5.0 V).

5.0 means that you have read the scale carefully and you are sure that the reading is closer to the 5 position than it is to 4.9 or 5.1.

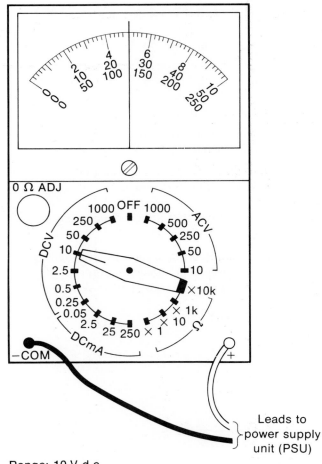

Range: 10 V d.c.
Scale to be read: 0 − 10
Reading: 5.0 V

A multimeter, or testmeter

For these testmeters, what
ranges have been selected
and what are the readings?

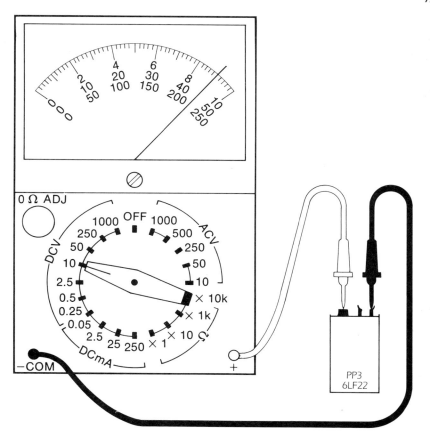

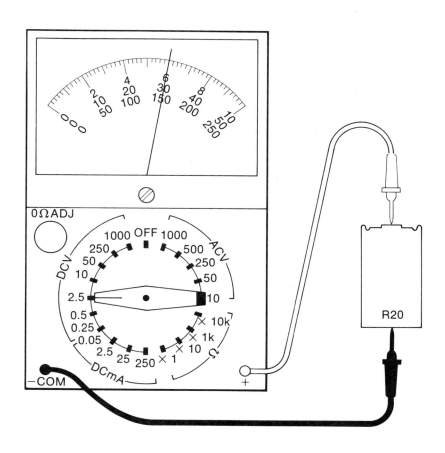

How we think of voltage in electronics

Think of **voltage** as **electrical height**.

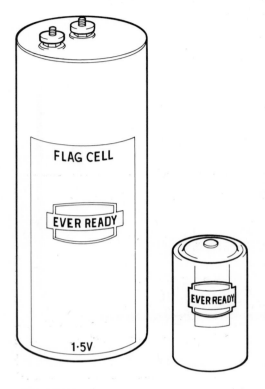

Flag cell and SP2/HP2

These are $1\frac{1}{2}$ V cells. This means that the positive terminal of each cell is $1\frac{1}{2}$ volts higher than the negative terminal.

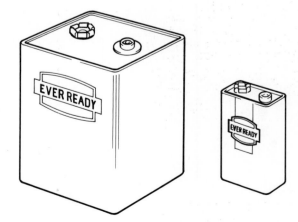

PP9 and PP3 batteries

These are 9 V batteries. The positive terminal of each battery is 9 volts higher than the negative terminal.

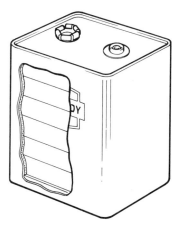

Cells of a PP9

PP3s and PP9s are 9 V batteries, because they contain six $1\frac{1}{2}$ V cells.

A PP9 is bigger than a PP3 but it has the same voltage so it will operate the same circuits.

A big battery contains more chemicals than a small one, therefore it can keep a circuit working for longer.

A PP9 costs a little more than a PP3 but it is better value for money because it can keep a circuit working for much longer.

Getting electricity from the mains (the Electricity Board's supply) is very much cheaper than getting it from batteries. One penny worth of electricity from the mains would cost hundreds of pence from small size batteries.

Prototype board

Prototype board (or breadboard)

The photograph shows a **prototype board**. Some people call it a **breadboard**. It enables you to build a circuit quickly, change it if you are not satisfied with the way it works, and finally recover the components in perfect condition for using again.

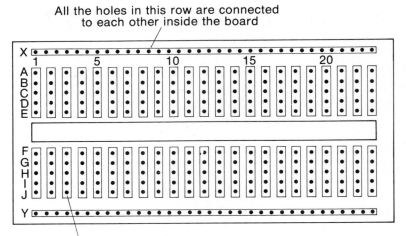

All the holes in this row are connected
to each other inside the board

The five holes in this half column are
connected to each other inside the board

Each hole ends with a metal clip that you cannot see without damaging
the board. The metal clips are connected to each other to make the rib-
like pattern shown above.

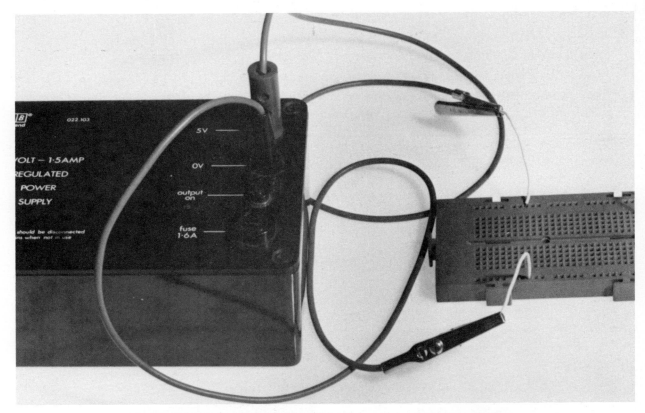

A 5 V power supply unit connected to a prototype board via plug-croc leads and connectors

This photograph shows how to connect a **power supply unit** (or a
battery) to a prototype board. The top row of holes is called the **positive
line** because they are all connected to the power supply's positive
terminal. The bottom row of holes is called the **negative line** because
they are all connected to the power supply's negative terminal.

Using resistors to create other electrical heights

The electrical height of the negative line is called 0 V (zero volts). It is like an electrical sea level. If we are using a 5 V power supply, the electrical height of the positive line will be 5 V.

One use of resistors is to create other electrical heights that are above zero but below the positive line voltage.

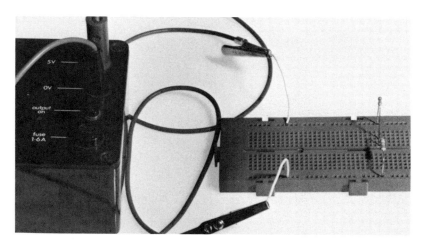
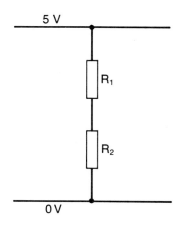

A 5 V power supply unit connected to a prototype board, with two resistors connected to form a voltage divider

The photograph shows how to use two resistors to create a point of connection whose electrical height is between 0 V and 5 V. The diagram on the right is the **circuit diagram**. Notice:

- the power supply (or the battery) is not usually included in the circuit diagram,
- the positive and negative line voltages should be included,
- a dot is used to show that a T junction has been formed,
- individual resistors should be given names . . . R_1, etc.

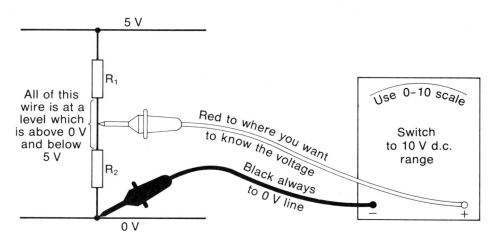

Using a testmeter to measure voltages

Cliff drawings to show voltages

This circuit is like a cliff that goes down to the sea in two huge steps. The width of the ledge does not matter. All that matters is the heights of the two steps.

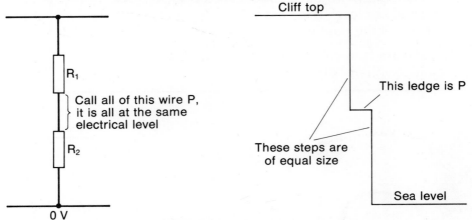

If the voltage at P is half of the positive line voltage, R_1 and R_2 have the same **resistance**.

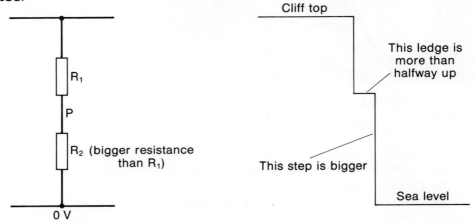

If the voltage at P is over half of the positive line voltage, the resistance of R_2 is bigger than the resistance of R_1.

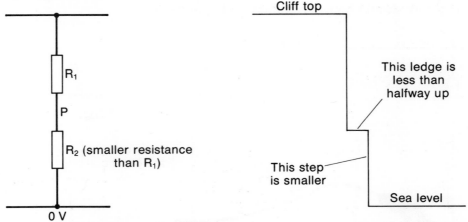

If the voltage at P is less than half of the positive line voltage, the resistance of R_2 is less than the resistance of R_1.

Practical tests with resistors

Doing these tests gives you useful practice with a testmeter, prepares you for building your first proper circuit, and helps you towards understanding voltage. You have to follow these steps.

1 Connect a prototype board to a battery or power supply unit.

2 Make a circuit with the first pair of resistors in the R_1 and R_2 positions.

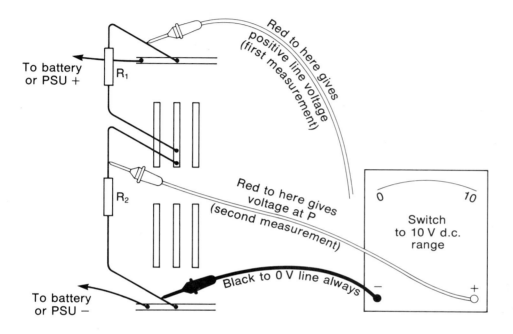

3 Measure the positive line voltage (testmeter negative to the negative line, testmeter positive to the positive line).

4 Measure the voltage where the resistors join (testmeter negative still to negative line, testmeter positive to where the resistors join).

5 Enter the figures in your data table.

6 Repeat for the other pairs of resistors.

Data table

R_1			R_2			Positive line voltage	Voltage at P	What can be worked out about the resistances of R_1 and R_2
brown	black	red	brown	black	red			
brown	green	red	brown	black	red			
brown	black	red	brown	green	red			

7 Do cliff drawings to illustrate each situation. For example, the first drawing might look like this. It should be constructed carefully using the blue lines of your writing paper as one volt steps.

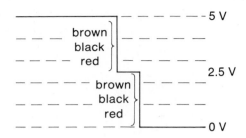

If you have time, you could try using three resistors to make a three-step cliff. Measure the heights of both ledges and do the cliff drawing to scale.

Using the resistor colour code

black	= 0
brown	= 1
red	= 2
orange	= 3
yellow	= 4
green	= 5
blue	= 6
violet	= 7
grey	= 8
white	= 9

Resistances are measured in ohms (Ω)

$\qquad$ or kilohms (kΩ)

$\qquad$ or megohms (MΩ)

$$1 k\Omega = 1000 \ \Omega$$

$$1 M\Omega = 1\,000\,000 \ \Omega$$

Most resistors have four coloured bands. The set of four is nearer to one end than to the other end. Hold a resistor so that the end nearest the bands is to your left.

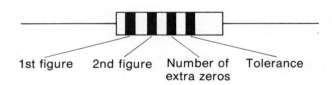

1st figure   2nd figure   Number of   Tolerance
$\qquad\qquad\qquad\qquad\qquad$ extra zeros

The tolerance band just tells you how accurate the resistance value is. Ignore it for now.

Some examples

brown black red	= 1000 Ω (1 then 0 then two extra zeroes) = 1 kΩ
brown black yellow	= 100 000 Ω (1 then 0 then four extra zeros) = 100 kΩ
orange orange orange	= 33 000 Ω (3 then 3 then three extra zeros) = 33 kΩ
brown green green	= 1 500 000 Ω = 1.5 MΩ

2.7 kΩ = 2700 Ω = red violet red

100 Ω = brown black brown

10 Ω = brown black black (1 then 0 then **no** extra zeros)

Questions

(Read p. 100 before answering questions 1 to 5.)

1 What do we mean when we say that an SP2 is a $1\frac{1}{2}$ volt cell?

2 How many cells does a $4\frac{1}{2}$ V flat-pack battery contain?

3 Why is a big $1\frac{1}{2}$ V cell better value for money than a small $1\frac{1}{2}$ V cell?

4 Suppose you have a portable radio which can be operated from the mains or from batteries. Why should you run it with mains electricity whenever you can?

5 Suppose you have a portable radio that is normally run by a PP3 battery. What is the advantage and the disadvantage of using a PP9 instead of a PP3?

6 The diagram shows the d.c. voltage scales of a testmeter.

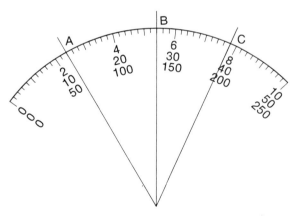

(a) If the 10 V d.c. range has been selected, what voltages are indicated by the pointer positions A, B and C?

(b) (Difficult) If the 2.5 V d.c. range had been selected, the $\frac{10}{50}{250}$ position would represent 2.5 V. What voltages would then be indicated by the pointer positions A, B and C?

7 Draw a diagram to show the d.c. voltage scales of a testmeter. If the 10 V d.c. range had been selected, draw pointer positions to indicate 1.5 V, 3.0 V and 8.8 V.

8 What use of resistors is described on p. 103?

9 What resistance values are represented by:
 (a) brown black orange
 (b) brown black green
 (c) yellow violet yellow
 (d) brown black yellow
 (e) brown black red
 (f) red red orange
 (g) orange orange orange
 (h) orange white red
 (i) brown grey blue
 (j) yellow violet black?

10 (a) How big is step (a)?

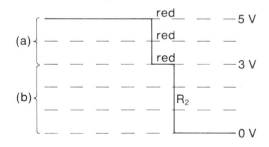

(b) How big is step (b)?
(c) What colour code would you need for R_2? Give your reasons.

Harder questions

11 What is the colour code for
 (a) 680 Ω   (e) 680 kΩ   (i) 1.5 MΩ
 (b) 100 Ω   (f) 33 Ω   (j) 10 MΩ?
 (c) 47 kΩ   (g) 3.3 kΩ
 (d) 100 kΩ   (h) 8.2 kΩ

A formula for calculating step heights

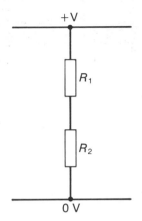

We have used R_1 and R_2 to stand for the **names** of the two resistors. We shall now use R_1 and R_2 to stand for their resistance values.

$R_1 + R_2$ stands for the combined resistance value.

The formula for calculating the step height across R_2 is:

$$\text{step height} = \frac{R_2}{R_1 + R_2} \text{ times the positive line voltage}$$

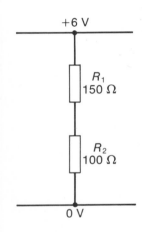

In this arrangement,

$$R_1 = 150 \ \Omega$$
$$R_2 = 100 \ \Omega$$
$$R_1 + R_2 = 250 \ \Omega$$
$$\text{Step height} = \frac{100 \ \Omega}{250 \ \Omega} \times 6 \text{ V}$$
$$= \underline{\underline{2.4 \text{ V}}}$$

---

12 Use the formula to calculate the step height across R_2 for each of these arrangements.

(a) 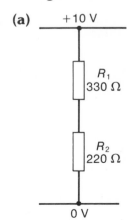 **(b)** 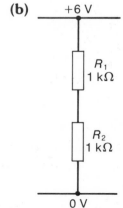 **(c)** 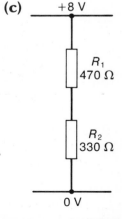 **(d)**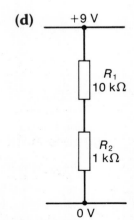

6 Generating and using a voltage pattern

Suppose you want to switch something on and off repeatedly, such as a bleeping siren or flashing lights at a pedestrian crossing. You need to generate a voltage pattern. That is what the pulse generator circuit in this chapter does.

555 Timer IC

A **silicon chip** is a tiny slice of an element called **silicon** into which an electronic circuit has been built. It is only about 1 mm square. This is too small to handle, so it is enclosed in plastic with gold wires connecting it to pins. The complete package is called an **integrated circuit** (or **IC** for short).

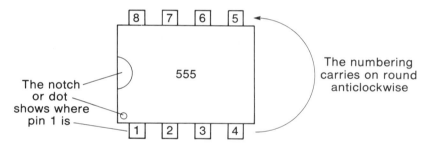

A 555 can be used to control the times when other things are switched on and off, so its full name is a **555 timer**. The chip inside it contains 22 transistors, 2 diodes and 16 resistors.

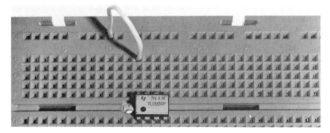

Prototype board with a 555 IC in place; pin 8 is connected to top line

Notice two things in the photograph:
- the 555 is placed across the central channel of the board,
- the wire connects pin 8 to the positive line and does it in the best possible way.

To connect one end of the wire to pin 8 you could use any of the four empty holes that are connected to the pin 8 hole. By using the hole that is furthest from the IC you keep the board clear for more components.

Building a pulse generator

1   Check that you have the following:
   - prototype board and 555
   - 4 connectors (6 cm lengths of 1/0.6 mm equipment wire with their ends stripped),
   - capacitor, 2.2 μF (C) [μF is short for microfarad],

The − signs indicate
the negative lead

   - resistor, brown black orange (R_1),
   - resistor, brown black green (R_2).

2   Straighten all the wires. Eventually when you have to bend a wire, do it across a thumb nail so that you make a right angle bend.

3   Check the position of pin 1 on the IC.

4   Build the circuit by following this drawing.

5   Have your wiring checked before testing the circuit.

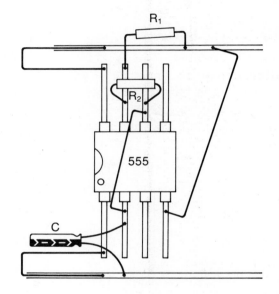

Testing the circuit

Before connecting the circuit to a battery or power supply unit (PSU)

1   (a)   Switch a testmeter to its 10 V d.c. range.
     (b)   Make sure that the red lead is in the **+** socket and the black lead is in the **−** socket.
     (c)   Measure the voltage of the battery or PSU. 9 V is a good voltage on which to operate this circuit, but you could use a 5 V PSU or a $4\frac{1}{2}$ V flatpack battery.

2   Connect the battery or PSU to the **+** and **−** lines of your circuit.

3   Check that the 555 is powered correctly by connecting testmeter **+** to pin 8 and **−** to pin 1. **If the voltage reading is less than the battery or PSU voltage which you measured, switch off immediately and have your circuit checked.**

4   If everything is all right so far, connect testmeter **+** to pin 3 and **−** to pin 1. The pointer should jump, stay, drop, stay, over and over again.

The pulse generator circuit diagram

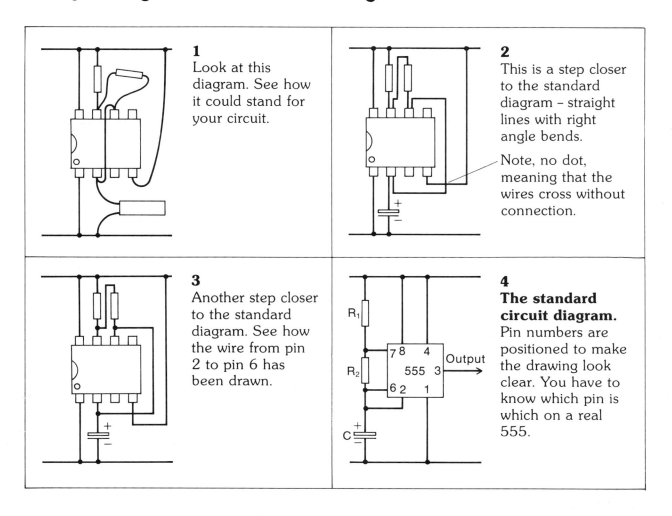

1 Look at this diagram. See how it could stand for your circuit.

2 This is a step closer to the standard diagram – straight lines with right angle bends.

Note, no dot, meaning that the wires cross without connection.

3 Another step closer to the standard diagram. See how the wire from pin 2 to pin 6 has been drawn.

4 **The standard circuit diagram.** Pin numbers are positioned to make the drawing look clear. You have to know which pin is which on a real 555.

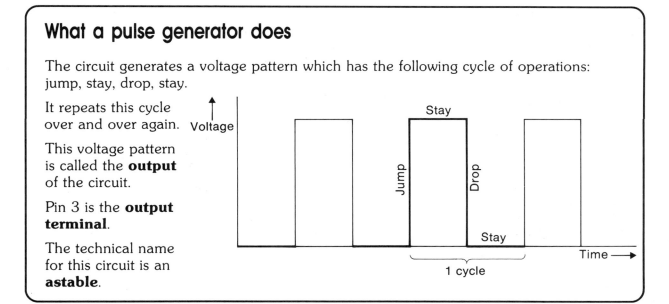

What a pulse generator does

The circuit generates a voltage pattern which has the following cycle of operations: jump, stay, drop, stay.

It repeats this cycle over and over again.

This voltage pattern is called the **output** of the circuit.

Pin 3 is the **output terminal**.

The technical name for this circuit is an **astable**.

How the pulse generator's output can be used

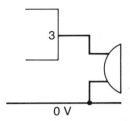

A buzzer can be connected between pin 3 and the negative line. The **pulse generator's output** (i.e. the voltage pattern at pin 3) is the **input to the buzzer**. The buzzer is on whenever its input is high; it is off whenever its input is low. A buzzer which bleeps (i.e. one which is continually turning on and off) is a more effective alarm than one which is on all the time.

       is the symbol for a buzzer.

How the pulse generator's output can be controlled

Controlling the output of a pulse generator means controlling the time it takes to generate each cycle of the voltage pattern. This time is controlled by the size of the capacitor and the resistance of the two resistors.

1   Build the circuit using $R_1 = 10\ \text{k}\Omega$, $R_2 = 1\ \text{M}\Omega$ and $C = 2.2\ \mu\text{F}$.

2   Prepare to record your data.

Controlling the Pulse Generator's Output

Capacitor Control

Capacitor	Time for 20 Cycles
2.2 µF	
1 µF	
0.1 µF	

3   Measure the time for 20 cycles (i.e. time 20 bleeps) and enter it in your table.

4   Replace the 2.2 µF capacitor by a 1 µF capacitor. Time 20 cycles and enter the time in your table.

5   Replace the 1 µF by a 0.1 µF capacitor. Time 20 cycles (you may have to practise this) and enter the time in your table.

6   1 µF is about half of 2.2 µF. Check that the second time is about half of the first, i.e. check that **halving the value of C causes the time to be halved**.

7 0.1 µF is one tenth of 1 µF. Check that the third time is about one tenth of the second.

8 Return to $C = 2.2$ µF and then time 20 cycles using different resistors in the R_2 position. Record your data as shown here.

Resistor Control Using R_2

R_2	Time for 20 Cycles
1MΩ	
470kΩ	
220kΩ	

9 470 kΩ is about half of 1 MΩ. 220 kΩ is about half of 470 kΩ. Check that your data shows that **halving the value of R_2 causes the time to be halved**.

How the timing control works

The three timing components and the battery or power supply unit (PSU) form a simple circuit. The point to think about in the circuit is where R_2 meets C.

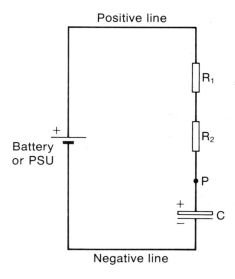

See what happens with the values shown here.

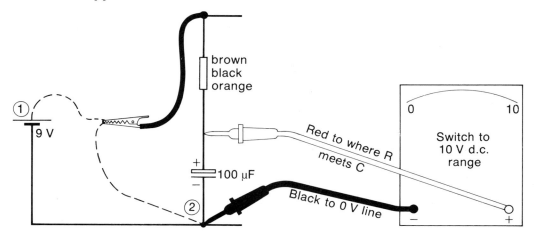

1 Fix the connecting lead to the battery's positive terminal①. The pointer of the testmeter moves steadily across the scale. This shows that **the voltage across the capacitor rises steadily**, i.e. **the capacitor charges up**.

2 Move the connecting lead to the negative line ②. The testmeter now shows that the **voltage across the capacitor falls steadily**, i.e. **the capacitor discharges**.

3 Try using a capacitor which is twice as big (220 μF) or a resistor which has twice the resistance (red-red-orange). You will see that the pointer takes twice as long to rise and fall.

The circuit inside the 555 causes C to be charged and discharged repeatedly, but the time it takes to do this is controlled by R_1, R_2 and C, not by the 555.

> A variety of different voltage patterns are used in a very large number of electronic systems, particularly in music synthesisers. One of the main uses of resistors and capacitors is to control the time it takes to generate individual cycles in the voltage patterns.

Other ways of using a pulse generator's output

Instead of a buzzer, a counting circuit could be connected to pin 3 so that the output of the pulse generator is the input to the counter. If the generator produces one cycle every second, the counter tells you the number of seconds that the generator is switched on.

If you could arrange for the generator to be switched on and off by a moving vehicle you could set up a **speed trap**. With the units studied in Chapter 1, this system might work.

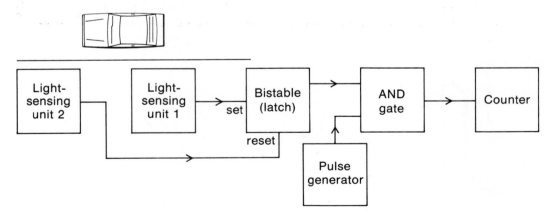

If you could arrange for a pulse generator to be switched on only when your **central heating system** was on, you could measure the time for which it was on. You might then be able to work out how much heat was being used.

Questions

1 What is a silicon chip?

2 What material is used to connect the pins to the chip inside an IC package?

3 How do you tell which is the negative lead on a capacitor?

4 Draw the following circuit diagram.
   (a) Draw **+** and **−** lines.
   (b) Draw a square between them and label it 555.
   (c) Connect pin 8 to the **+** line.
   (d) Connect pin 1 to the **−** line.
   (e) Connect pin 4 to the **+** line.
   (f) Connect pin 7 to pin 6 (with connecting wire, not a resistor).
   (g) Connect a resistor between pin 7 and the **+** line.
   (h) Connect a capacitor between pin 7 and the **−** line.

5 Draw **from memory** the standard circuit diagram of the pulse generator.

6 What is meant by the **output** of a pulse generator?

7 Describe in detail how you test the pulse generator, and say how you know if it is working.

8 The output of a buzzer is a sound pattern. What is its input?

9 What controls the time to generate each cycle of a pulse generator's output?

10 If your pulse generator made a buzzer produce two bleeps per second, how could you change it to produce four bleeps per second?

11 Describe **two** uses of resistors in electronic circuits. (One was described in Chapter 5.)

12 What do we mean in electronics when we say that a capacitor is being charged?

13 Read the section headed 'Other ways of using a pulse generator's output'.
   (a) If the pulse generator produced 1000 cycles every second instead of 1 cycle per second, what time would be indicated by a reading of 2746?
   (b) For use in a speed trap, would a high frequency pulse generator be better or worse than a low frequency pulse generator? Explain.

14 (Only if you have studied Chapter 1)
   (a) Try to explain how the speed trap system should work.
   (b) Try to work out a block diagram for the central heating timing system.

7 Gate combinations

Sometimes we want the output of a circuit to depend upon two things.

Example 1   An alarm should sound if the water level is too high **OR** if it is too low.

Example 2   An alarm should sound if the water level is too low **AND** it is not raining.

Gate circuits allow us to bring two (or more) inputs together.

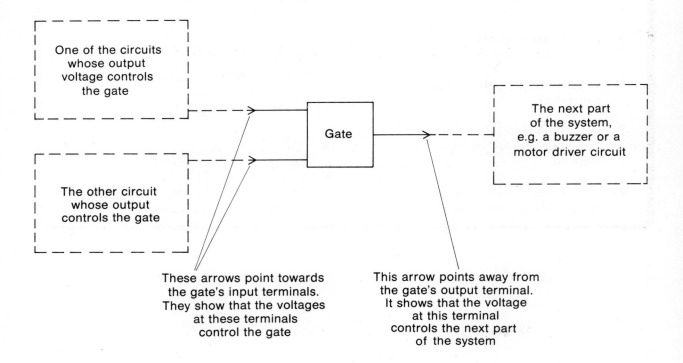

The circuit designer tries to ensure that a gate's input voltages are either high or low, and not at an in-between level.

High means at or near the voltage of the positive line.

Low means at or near the voltage of the negative line.

If there are two input terminals and each can be low voltage or high voltage, how many combinations are possible?

One input voltage	Other input voltage
low	low
low	high
high	low
high	high

A similar question: how many combinations are possible when two coins are tossed?

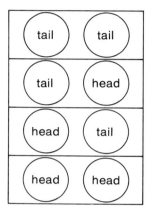

Whether it is two coins or two input voltages, there are **four** combinations.

Different types of gate respond differently to the four input combinations. One type of gate responds like this:

Voltage at one input terminal	Voltage at other input terminal	Voltage which the gate produces at its output terminal
low	low	low
low	high	high
high	low	high
high	high	high

You could put it like this: the output voltage is high if one input OR the other input is high. A gate of this type is called an **OR gate**.

The most common standard symbol for an OR gate is

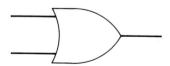

Information about OR gates and about some other types of gate is summarised in the following tables. The tables are called **truth tables**.

OR gate

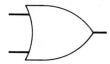

The output voltage is high if one input OR the other input is high.

One input voltage	Other input voltage	Output voltage the gate produces
low	low	low
low	high	high
high	low	high
high	high	high

AND gate

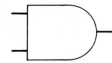

The output voltage is high only if one input AND the other input is high.

One input voltage	Other input voltage	Output voltage the gate produces
low	low	low
low	high	low
high	low	low
high	high	high

NOT gate

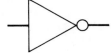

The output voltage is high if the input voltage is NOT high.

It is commonly called a **NOT gate** even though it has only one input. Its other common name is an **inverter**.

Input voltage	Output voltage the gate produces
low	high
high	low

Sometimes we want the output of a circuit to depend upon a complicated set of conditions.

Example 1   A door bolt is opened and closed using a control panel containing eight buttons, A to H. The bolt should be withdrawn if buttons A, D and F are pressed while buttons B, C, E, G and H are not pressed.

Example 2   An alarm should sound if a beam of light (or infra red, or ultrasound) is blocked and a similar beam is not blocked within the next two seconds.

Combinations of AND, OR and NOT gates allow almost any set of conditions to be met.

How to work out the behaviour of a set of gates

Suppose that you need to know how this combination will behave for each of the four possible input combinations. Proceed as follows:

1   Add letters to any connections that do not already have letters.

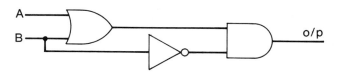

Notice that the input of the NOT gate must always be at the same voltage as the lower input of the OR gate so it is given the same letter.

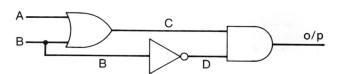

2   Draw an empty table with a column for each different letter. Put in the four possible input combinations.

3   Work out what goes in column C. To do this notice that C is the output of a

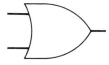

for which A and B are the inputs.

A	B	C	D	o/p
low	low			
low	high			
high	low			
high	high			

4   Work out what goes in column D. To do this notice that D is the output of a

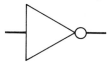

for which B is the input.
(So ignore the A and C columns while you fill this one in.)

A	B	C	D	o/p
low	low	low		
low	high	high		
high	low	high		
high	high	high		

5   Work out the final output column. To do this notice that it is the output of a

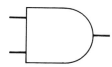

for which C and D are the inputs.

A	B	C	D	o/p
low	low	low	high	
low	high	high	low	
high	low	high	high	
high	high	high	low	

Your final answer should look like this.

A	B	C	D	o/p
low	low	low	high	low
low	high	high	low	low
high	low	high	high	high
high	high	high	low	low

Questions

1 A gate's input voltages must be either high or low. What does **high** mean in this sentence?

2

(a) Copy this diagram and add arrows so that P is the input terminal and Q is the output terminal.
(b) What does the voltage at P control?
(c) What does the voltage at Q control?

3 A gate's output voltage is high only when both input voltages are high. What type of gate is it?

4 A gate's output voltage is always low except when both input voltages are high. What type of gate is it?

5 A gate's output voltage is high only when both input voltages are low. Copy and complete the table for this gate.

One input voltage	Other input voltage	Output voltage the gate produces

6 A gate's output voltage is NOT high only if both input voltages are high. Draw the complete truth table for this gate. (It is called a NAND gate.)

7 What is an OR gate?

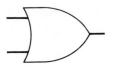

(Begin your answer like this: An OR gate is a circuit whose output voltage is high when . . .)

8 In each of these questions, one piece of information is missing. Decide what should go into the empty spaces.

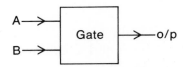

	Input A voltage	Input B voltage	Gate	Output voltage
(a)	low	low	AND	
(b)	low	low	OR	
(c)	low	high		high
(d)	high	high		high

9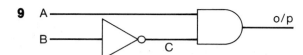

Copy and complete the truth table for this combination.

A	B	C	o/p
low	low		
low	high		
high	low		
high	high		

Ignore A when working out C.

Ignore B when working out the final output.

10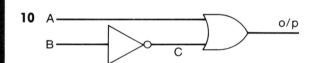

Copy and complete the truth table for this combination.

A	B	C	o/p
low	low		
low	high		
high	low		
high	high		

A	B	C	o/p 1	o/p 2
low	low			
low	high			
high	low			
high	high			

Copy and complete the truth table.

12 This circuit does a similar job to that of question 11. Details of how to use it are worked out at the end of Chapter 13.

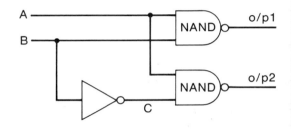

A	B	C	o/p 1	o/p 2

Copy and complete the truth table. Remember to use the NAND gate table that you worked out in question 6.

11 This circuit can control the direction of rotation of a motor and also turn the motor on and off.

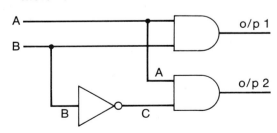

13 Work out the truth table for this combination.

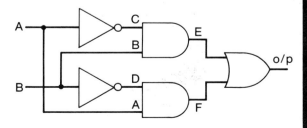

8 Using logic gate ICs

NAND gates are used more often than any other type of gate when
building electronic circuits. The reason is that all other gates can be made
by combining a few NAND gates, and this often allows us to use fewer ICs
in real applications.

The commonest standard symbol for a NAND gate is

The gate's input voltages should be high or low, not at an in-between
level. **High** means at or near the voltage of the positive line; **low** means at
or near the voltage of the negative line (0 V).

There are four possible combinations of input voltages.

1
low
low

2
low
high

3
high
low

4
high
high

The way that a NAND gate responds to these combinations is summarised
by its truth table.

NAND gate

The output voltage is NOT high only if
one input AND the other input are high.

(NAND is short for NOT AND.)

One input voltage	Other input voltage	Output voltage the gate produces
low	low	high
low	high	high
high	low	high
high	high	low

4011 IC package

The notch or dot shows where pin 1 is

4011

The numbering carries on round anticlockwise so pin 14 is opposite pin 1

A 4011 is a 14 pin IC package. The silicon chip inside it has four separate NAND gate circuits built into it. The chip itself is no bigger than the chip in a 555 but the common way to draw a 4011 is like this.

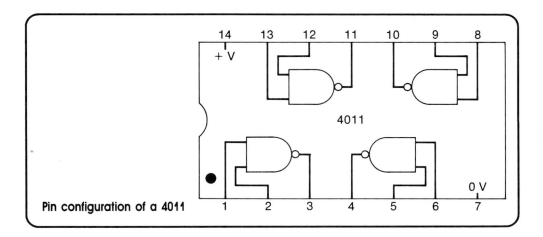

Pin configuration of a 4011

The drawing is called a **pin configuration** because it shows the internal connections between the pins and the chip. Notice that power has to be supplied to operate the circuits via pins 7 and 14.
- Pin 7 has to be connected to the negative line. It is like pin 1 of a 555.
- Pin 14 has to be connected to the positive line. It is like pin 8 of a 555.

Testing the NAND gates in a 4011

Testing the NAND gates means checking that they work according to the NAND gate pattern shown by the truth table on p. 122.

1 Build the test circuit shown at the top of the following page by following the circuit diagram if you can, otherwise follow the drawing.

2 Connect the battery or PSU to the **+** and **−** lines of your circuit.

3 Switch a testmeter to its 10 V d.c. range. Connect the testmeter **+** to the output terminal of the NAND gate (i.e. to pin 3) and **−** to pin 7 or anywhere on the negative line.

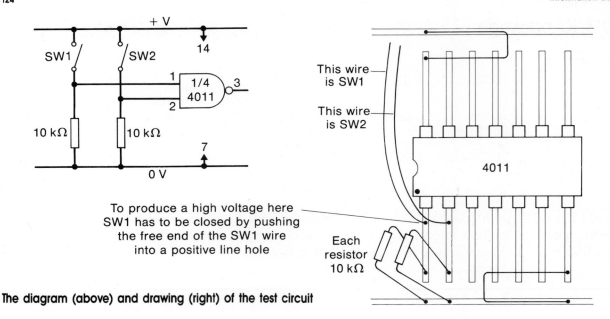

The diagram (above) and drawing (right) of the test circuit

To produce a high voltage here SW1 has to be closed by pushing the free end of the SW1 wire into a positive line hole

Each resistor 10 kΩ

4 Check that the NAND gate works like this.

(a) With the free ends of the SW1 and SW2 wires 'floating' in the air as shown in the drawing, both input voltages are low. The testmeter should show a high voltage at pin 3. (Does it, with your circuit?)

With both inputs at low voltage, output voltage is high.

(b) With **one** of the free ends pushed into a positive line hole, the testmeter should still show a high voltage at pin 3. (Does it, with your circuit?)

With one input at low voltage and the other at high voltage, output voltage is high.

(c) With **both** free ends pushed into positive lines holes, the testmeter should show low voltage at pin 3. (Does it, with your circuit?)

With both inputs at high voltage, output voltage is low.

5 Check at least one of the other three NAND gates, for example the one that goes to pins 8, 9 and 10. To do this, follow these steps.

(a) Move the two resistors and the SW1, SW2 wires to pins 8 and 9, as shown here.

(b) Connect testmeter **+** to the output terminal (pin 10) and **−** to pin 7.

(c) Repeat the tests described above in instruction 4 so that you test **all** of the possible input combinations.

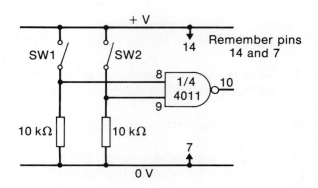

Combining two NAND gates to act like a different type of gate

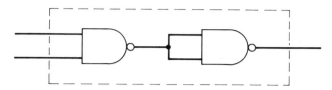

This combination of two NAND gates acts like a different type of gate.
To find out what it does, set up the following test arrangement.

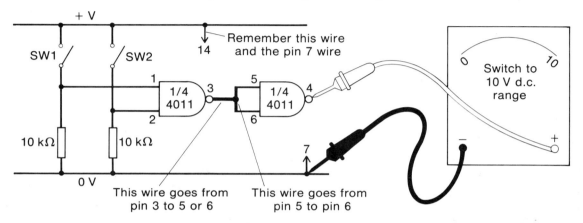

Find answers to the following questions.

(a) With the free ends of the SW 1 and SW 2 wires 'floating' in the air as
shown in the drawing on p. 124, both input voltages are low. Does the
testmeter show high or low voltage at the output terminal (pin 4)?

> **With both inputs at low voltage, output voltage is . . .**

(b) With **one** of the free ends pushed into a positive line hole, does the
testmeter show high or low voltage at pin 4?

> **With one input at low voltage and the other at high voltage,**
> **output voltage is . . .**

(c) With **both** free ends pushed into positive line holes, does the testmeter
show high or low voltage at pin 4?

> **With both inputs at high voltage, output voltage is . . .**

Does the combination follow the OR gate pattern on p. 118?

Does the combination follow the AND gate pattern on p. 118?

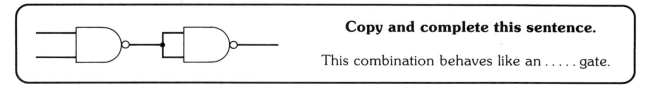

Copy and complete this sentence.

This combination behaves like an . . . . . gate.

Investigation of a three NAND gate combination

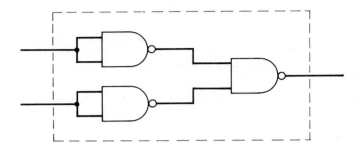

This is another useful NAND gate combination. To find out what it does,
set up the following test arrangement.

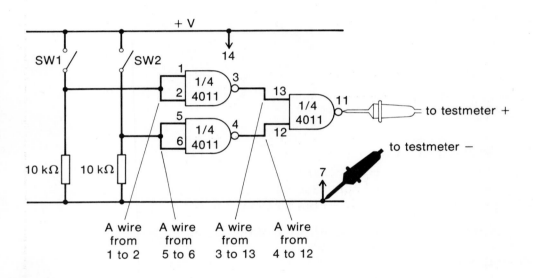

Notice that SW 2 and its resistor go to pin 5 or pin 6, not to pin 2.
See what the testmeter shows as you try out the four different
arrangements of SW 1 and SW 2. Does the combination follow the OR
gate pattern or the AND gate pattern?

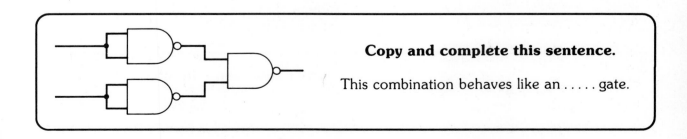

Copy and complete this sentence.

This combination behaves like an . . . . . gate.

Switch control

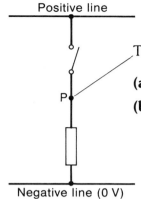

This point is connected to one of the input terminals of a gate.

(a) If the switch is open, P is at 0 V.

(b) If the switch is closed, P is at positive line voltage.

Closed switch produces high voltage at P.

The switch could be a reed switch that could be opened or closed by a magnet. Reed switches are described on p. 167.

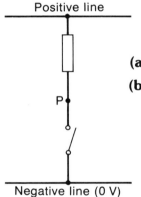

(a) If the switch is open, P is at positive line voltage.

(b) If the switch is closed, P is at 0 V.

Open switch produces high voltage at P.

Water level detection

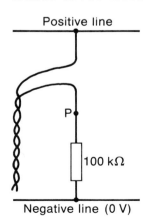

The 'switch' consists of two long pieces of connecting wire. When the bared ends dip into water the 'switch' is 'closed'.

However, water is a very poor connector so 100 kΩ resistors are needed to make the 'switch' work well enough.

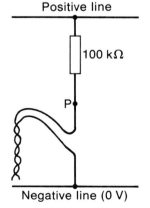

Ends **in water** produces high voltage at P

Ends **out of water** produces high voltage at P

Designing a circuit to solve a problem

The problem   An alarm should sound if the water level is too high OR if it is too low.

First decide what modules are likely to be needed and which should control which.
(1)   Buzzer to provide the alarm sound
(2)   High level water detector
(3)   Low level water detector
(4)   OR gate

They should be combined like this.

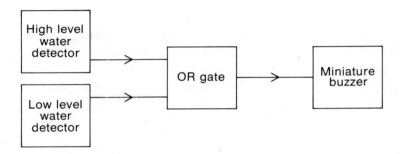

The arrows show what controls what.

The gate circuits in a 4011 are powerful enough to drive a miniature piezo-electric buzzer directly.

Then draw positive and negative lines and replace each named box by the circuit that will do its job.

This is rather like doing a jigsaw puzzle. All you are doing is finding the right pieces and connecting them in the right order.

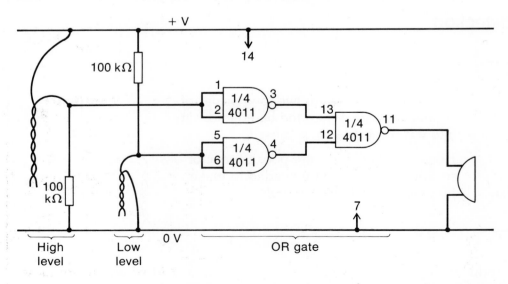

Build the circuit by following the circuit diagram if you can, otherwise follow the drawing on the opposite page. Make sure that it works as required.

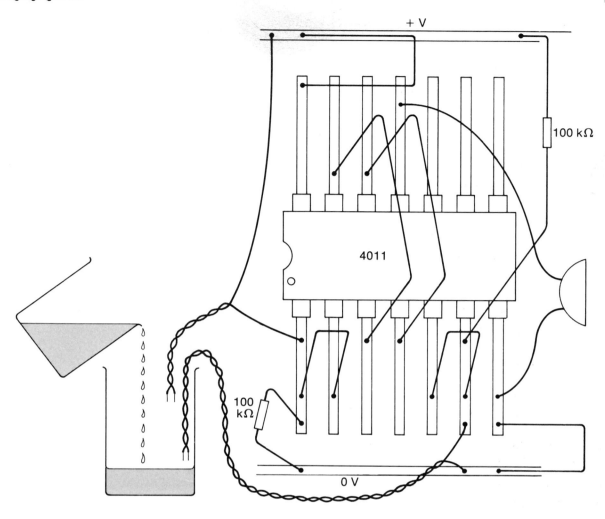

If you have time to spare see how this circuit works.

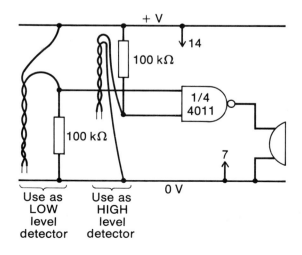

Use as LOW level detector

Use as HIGH level detector

Ways of including an inverter in a project system

1 Use a 4069. It contains six separate inverters.

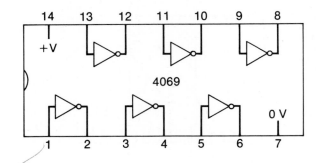

4069

2 Use a NAND gate with its inputs connected together.

$$\boxed{\begin{array}{c}1/4\\4011\end{array}}\quad\equiv\quad$$

3 Use a NOR gate with its inputs connected together.

$$\boxed{\begin{array}{c}1/4\\4001\end{array}}\quad\equiv\quad$$

4 Use a transistor switching circuit.

+V

1 kΩ

o/p

i/p 10 kΩ

0 V

$$\equiv$$

Any general purpose npn transistor will do.

Questions

1 In the circuit diagram at the bottom of p. 128, what does $\dfrac{7}{\text{0 V}}$ tell you to do?

2 What is the colour code for:
(a) 10 kΩ **(b)** 100 kΩ?

3

1/4 4011   1/4 4011

To join these two NAND gates together two connectors are needed. Would it be correct to put one from pin 3 to pin 5 and the other from pin 3 to pin 6? (If it is not correct, say why not.)

4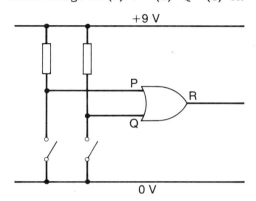

(a) Copy this diagram and add the four missing pin numbers.

(b) Say what connections are needed to make this combination.

5 If both of these switches are **closed**, what is the voltage at: **(a)** P   **(b)** Q   **(c)** R?

6 In each of these questions, one piece of information is missing. Decide what should go into the empty spaces.

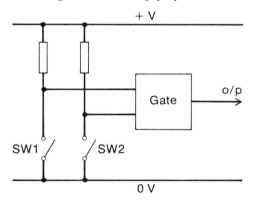

	SW 1	SW 2	Gate	Output voltage
(a)	open	open	OR	
(b)	closed	closed	AND	
(c)	open	open		low
(d)	open	closed		high

7 In each of these questions, one piece of information is missing. Decide what should go into the empty spaces.

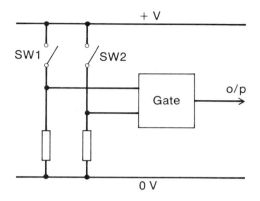

	SW 1	SW 2	Gate	Output voltage
(a)	open	open	NAND	
(b)	open	open	AND	
(c)	open	open	OR	
(d)	open	closed		low

8 Draw the combination of NAND gates that act as:
(a) an AND gate,
(b) an OR gate.

9 If you had a 4011 and you wanted to check that the gate that goes to pins 4, 5 and 6 was in working order, what should you do? Give detailed instructions for testing it.

9 Bistables and monostables

Compare these two switches in a burglar alarm system.

1 An ordinary switch   A burglar opens a window; an alarm turns on. The burglar closes the window; the alarm turns off.

2 A bistable switch   A burglar opens a window; an alarm turns on. The burglar closes the window; the alarm stays on until the householder resets the system using a different switch.

Bistable (latch) operation

The following set of diagrams shows the electrical operation of a bistable switch or latch. The input terminals are called **set** and **reset**.

Both inputs are low. The output may be high or low. It depends what happened last at the inputs.

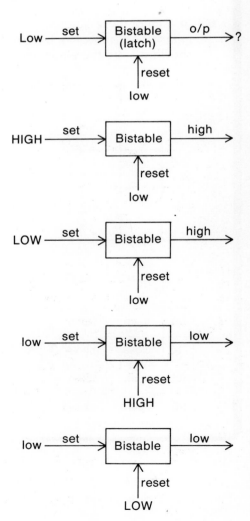

Step 1   If the set input goes high, the output goes high (or stays high if it was high already).

Step 2   If the set input goes low again, the output stays high. (Alarm stays on when burglar closes window.)

Step 3   If the reset input goes high, the output goes low. (Householder presses the reset button.)

Step 4   If the reset input goes low, the output stays low. (Householder releases the reset button.)

The simplest way to build a bistable is to use two NOR gates from a 4001.

NOR gate

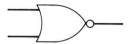

The output voltage is NOT high if one input OR the other input is high.

(NOR is short for NOT OR.)

One input voltage	Other input voltage	Output voltage the gate produces
low	low	high
low	high	low
high	low	low
high	high	low

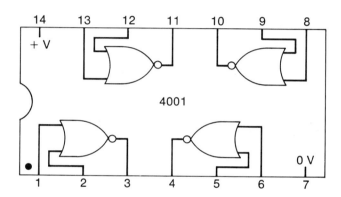

4001

Pin configuration of a 4001

The NOR gate bistable or latch

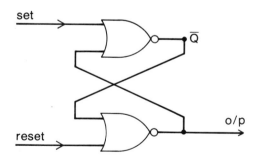

(When the output is high, $\overline{Q}$ is low. When the output is low, $\overline{Q}$ is high. You may find a use for the $\overline{Q}$ output in a project.)

Summary of bistable operation

To produce a high voltage output, the set input must go high.

To produce a low voltage output, the reset input must go high.

Set and reset will do their job only if the other input is low.

NAND gate bistables are described on p. 135.

Diodes

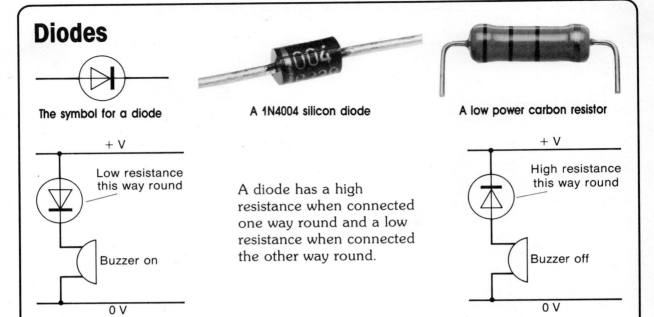

The symbol for a diode

A 1N4004 silicon diode

A low power carbon resistor

+ V

Low resistance
this way round

Buzzer on

0 V

A diode has a high
resistance when connected
one way round and a low
resistance when connected
the other way round.

+ V

High resistance
this way round

Buzzer off

0 V

A diode is the electronic equivalent of a tyre valve. Both of them allow
something to flow through in one direction only.

Light-emitting diodes (LEDs)

The symbol for an LED

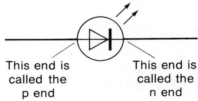

This end is
called the
p end

This end is
called the
n end

Emit means give out. An LED will emit
light if its p end is 1.7 V higher than its n
end.

A resistor is needed to protect an LED. It
has to make sure that the voltage drop
across the LED is not too big.

A red LED lights up well with a 1 kΩ
resistor and a 9 V supply.

LEDs can be used to monitor voltages in
gate circuits.

+ V

(1 kΩ
if + V
= 9 V)   Protective
resistor

p

LED on

n

n

LED off

p

0 V

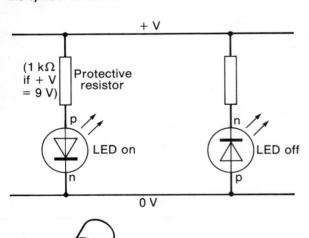

Straight here
indicates the
n wire

(thicker wire is n when case has no flat part)

Investigating the action of a bistable

1 Build the following test circuit.

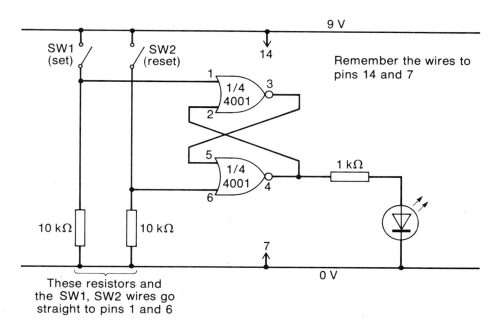

9 V

SW1
(set)

SW2
(reset)

14

Remember the wires to
pins 14 and 7

1

1/4
4001

3

2

5

1/4
4001

4

1 kΩ

6

10 kΩ

10 kΩ

7

0 V

These resistors and
the SW1, SW2 wires go
straight to pins 1 and 6

2 Check that the wires to pins 14 and 7 are in place. You are likely to
burn out the IC if you switch on before these are in place.

3 Check that the SW 2 wire and its resistor go to pin 6, not pin 2.

4 You could use another 1 kΩ resistor and LED to monitor the voltage
at pin 3. Whenever one LED is on, the other should be off.

5 Connect a 9 V supply and switch on.

6 Use the SW1 and SW2 wires to follow the steps on p. 132. Check that
the output does what it should do.

NAND gate bistables

Some manufactured bistable (latch)
modules are built using NAND gates. Set
and reset work by going **low**, and they do
their job only if the other input is high.

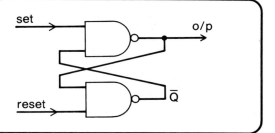

set

o/p

reset

$\bar{Q}$

Single pulse generator or monostable

Suppose that you have switched on a staircase light in a block of flats. You want to go away from the switch knowing that the light will turn off automatically two minutes later. This circuit will do the timing job for you.

Single pulse generator or monostable or one-shot

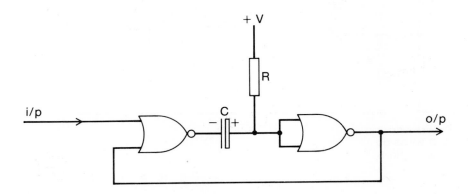

The circuit works like this:

1 When the input voltage goes high, the output voltage goes high.

2 The output voltage stays high for a time which is fixed by the values of R and C, after which it automatically goes low.

3 High time in seconds $\approx 0.7 \times R$ in megohms $\times C$ in microfarads.

$\approx$ means 'is approximately equal to'.

For example, if $R = 1\ M\Omega$ and $C = 1\ \mu F$,

high time $\approx 0.7 \times 1 \times 1$ seconds
≈ 0.7 seconds.

If $R = 10\ M\Omega$ and $C = 100\ \mu F$,

high time $\approx 0.7 \times 10 \times 100$ seconds
≈ 700 seconds

which is about 12 minutes.

Questions

1 What condition is necessary for an LED to emit light? (See p. 134.)

2 Which of these LEDs will be on?

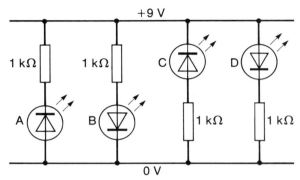

3 Which of these LEDs will be on? (Assume that the gate circuits are powered correctly.) Use the truth tables on p. 118 to work out the gate output before thinking about the LED.

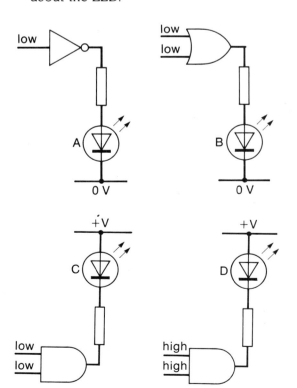

4 Which of these buzzers will be on? (Assume that the gate circuits are powered correctly so that they can drive a miniature buzzer directly.)

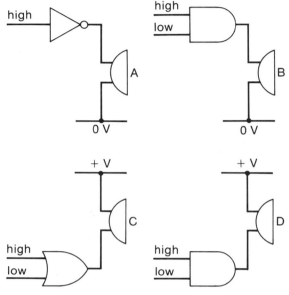

5 Here is a block diagram of part of a burglar alarm system.

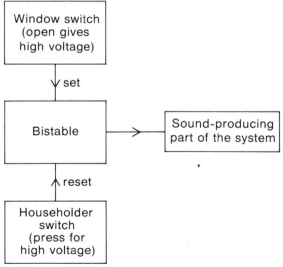

Most houses have more than one window. Suppose that there are just two windows and the system has to operate if one window OR the other is opened. Draw the block diagram for the new system.

6 The water level in a tank has to be kept between fixed limits. If the level becomes too low, a pump must turn on **and remain on** until the water reaches the upper level.

The system could include these modules.

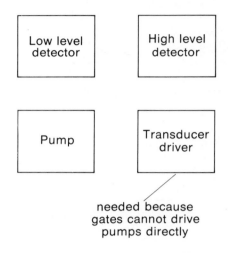

needed because
gates cannot drive
pumps directly

(a) One extra module is needed. Decide what it is, then draw the block diagram for the system.

(b) Which of the water level detectors on p. 127 would you use as the low level detector, and which would you use as the high level detector? Give the reasons for your choices.

7 Read example 1 on p. 118.
To satisfy the stated requirements you could use eight identical switch control units like this one.

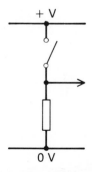

You would also need a few

and an 8-input AND gate:

See if you can draw the combination of switches and gates. (It could be built using the 8-input NAND gate in a 4068 and some of the inverters in a 4069.)

8 Read the section on the single pulse generator, p. 136.
   (a) With $R = 100$ kΩ and $C = 100$ µF, calculate the time that the output voltage stays high.
   (b) To produce a pulse lasting about two minutes, what R and C values could you use?

9 (Using two single pulse generators to produce a delayed pulse)

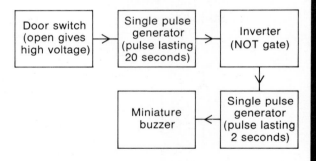

   (a) State precisely what the first pulse generator in this system does (and when it does it).
   (b) What does the second pulse generator do, and when does it do it?
   (c) Why is the inverter needed?
   (d) In relation to the opening or closing of the door, when is the buzzer on?

10 Counting and timing

Ways of counting

In everyday life we count in **tens**. We use ten different figures 0, 1, 2, 3, 4, 5, 6, 7, 8 and 9. We write numbers in rows; each figure would count for ten times as much as the same figure on its right.

Everyday (decimal) counting
factors of ten ⟶

	Thousands (10 × 100)	Hundreds (10 × 10)	Tens (10 × 1)	Units (1)
three =				3
eleven =			1	1
forty-four =			4	4
five hundred and ten =		5	1	0

To use electric circuits we have to count in **twos**. We must use only two figures 0 and 1. We must show big numbers in rows where each 1 counts for twice as much as a 1 on its right.

Binary counting
factors of two ⟶

	Hundred and twenty-eights (2 × 64)	Sixty-fours (2 × 32)	Thirty-twos (2 × 16)	Sixteens (2 × 8)	Eights (2 × 4)	Fours (2 × 2)	Twos (2 × 1)	Units (1)
one =								1
two =							1	0
three =							1	1
four =						1	0	0
five =						1	0	1
six =						1	1	0
seven =						1	1	1
eight =					1	0	0	0
nine =					1	0	0	1
ten =					1	0	1	0
eleven =					1	0	1	1
twelve =					1	1	0	0
thirteen =					1	1	0	1
fourteen =					1	1	1	0
fifteen =					1	1	1	1
sixteen =				1	0	0	0	0
one hundred and twenty-seven =		1	1	1	1	1	1	1
one hundred and twenty-eight =	1	0	0	0	0	0	0	0
two hundred and fifty-five =	1	1	1	1	1	1	1	1

Each 0 or 1 in a binary number is called a **bit**. 'Bit' is short for **binary digit**.

How an electronic counter counts

A 4024 is an IC package which contains a binary counter. The following circuit will show how it can be used to count.

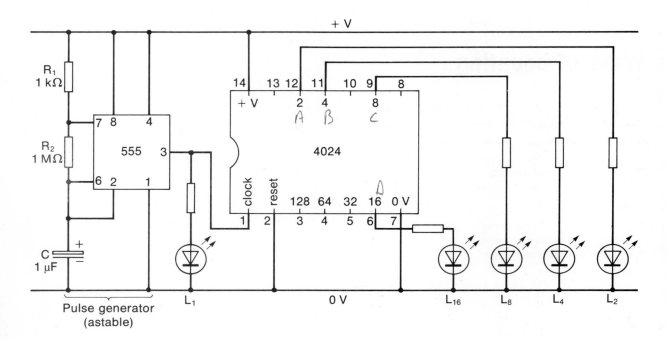

The astable produces the voltage waveform shown on p. 111. L_1 turns on when the voltage jumps and off when it drops. By watching L_1 you can count the number of cycles which reach the input terminal of the 4024 (pin 1, called the **clock terminal**).

When the astable produces the fifth cycle the LEDs look like this:

L_{16}	L_8	L_4	L_2	L_1
off	off	on	off	on

On the eleventh cycle they look like this:

L_{16}	L_8	L_4	L_2	L_1
off	on	off	on	on

The 4024 adds one to its output count each time its input voltage falls.

To count more than thirty-one cycles you need to put LEDs and resistors on pins, 3, 4 and 5.[†]

If the voltage at pin 2 is made to go high, the voltage at all of the output pins goes low. This is called **resetting** the counter.

[†]To count numbers greater than one hundred and twenty-seven, you could use a 4020 IC package (see p. 11).

How to produce a timed sequence of events

Example 1

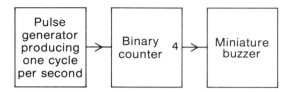

The buzzer will be on for all binary numbers which have a 1 in the 'fours' position:

> four, five, six, seven,
>
> twelve, thirteen, fourteen, fifteen,
>
> twenty, twenty-one, twenty-two, twenty-three,
>
> and so on.

Therefore the buzzer will be

> off for the first four seconds,
>
> on for the next four seconds,
>
> off for four seconds
>
> on for four seconds,
>
> and so on.

Example 2

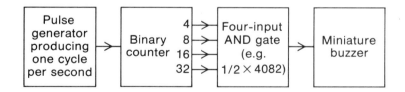

The AND gate's output will go high when the counter has received sixty cycles. It will go low again after four more cycles have reached the counter.

Therefore the buzzer will be

> off for the first sixty seconds,
>
> on for the next four seconds,

and this cycle will be repeated indefinitely.

Questions

1 Convert the following binary numbers into everyday (decimal) form.

10001   11010   101000

2 Write the following numbers in binary form.

fourteen
twenty-three
twenty-seven
sixty-six

3 For each of the following systems state as **precisely as possible** when the buzzer will be **on**.

(a)

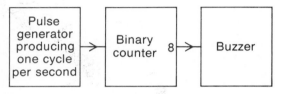

(b)

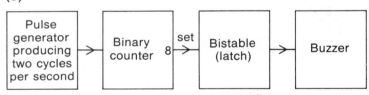

(c)

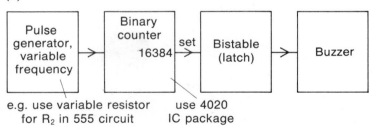

(d)

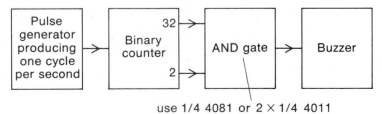

(e)

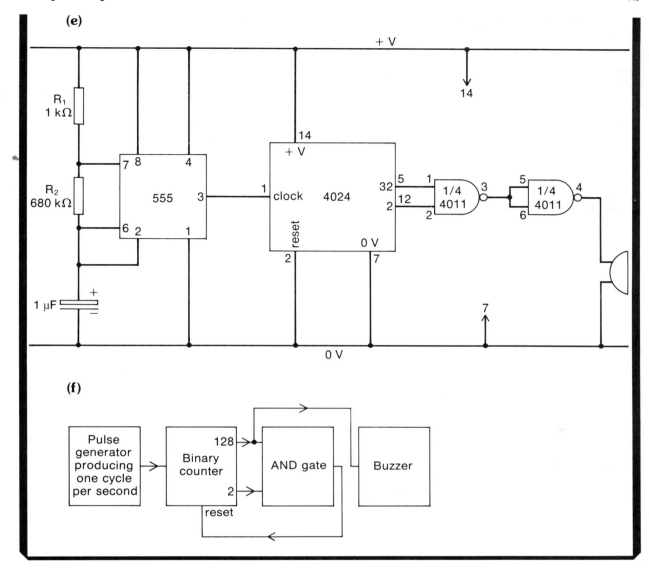

(f)

11 Sensors and input units

Getting information into electronic systems

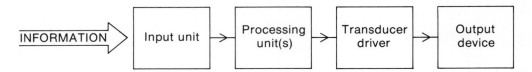

Arrows on block diagrams show what is controlling what. They also show the direction in which **information** passes through the system.

The information can arrive in different forms, which have nothing to do with either words or pictures. It could be a pattern of light levels, a pattern of pressure variations, and so on. In whatever form the information arrives, **the job of the input unit is to convert it into a voltage pattern**.

Switch unit

Temperature-sensing unit

Light-sensing unit

Input voltage unit

Each of these input units contains a **sensor**. A sensor is a component which can receive and respond to non-electrical information.
The first three input units each contain a resistor. The combination of sensor and resistor produces the voltage pattern.

We first study each sensor on its own before analysing a complete input unit.

Transducers

A **transducer** is a component which converts energy into a different form.

All sensors are transducers. For example, an LDR converts light energy into electrical energy. A thermistor converts heat energy into electrical energy.

All output devices are transducers. For example, a motor converts electrical energy into kinetic energy. A buzzer converts electrical energy into sound energy.

Light-dependent resistor (LDR)

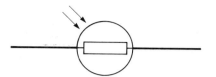

The symbol for an LDR

An ORP12, one of the most popular LDRs

An LDR is a component whose resistance can change depending upon the amount of light falling on it.

- More light makes the resistance decrease.
- Less light makes the resistance increase.

MORE
light

makes

lower
resistance

With the arrangement shown here you find that:

(1) When the top surface of the LDR is covered by a book or a coat, the resistance is bigger than a million ohms. (Scale reading 1 k × 1 kΩ range = 1 MΩ.)

(2) When the LDR is exposed to normal daylight, the resistance is in the region of a thousand ohms. (Scale reading 1 × 1 kΩ range = 1 kΩ.)

(3) When the LDR receives light from a bright lamp the resistance can be much less than 1 kΩ.

(4) With your finger over the LDR the resistance may be much less than 1 MΩ. Quite a lot of light can get through your finger.

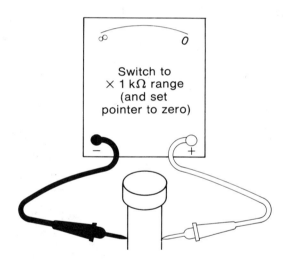

Switch to × 1 kΩ range (and set pointer to zero)

Switch

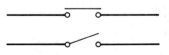

The symbols for a switch

When a switch is open, its resistance is infinite (too large to be measured). When it is closed, the resistance is zero.

A switch is a component whose resistance changes depending upon whether there is pressure on the 'button' or not.

Thermistor

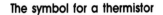

The symbol for a thermistor

An RA53 (bead type) thermistor

A VA1066S (rod type) thermistor

A thermistor is a component whose resistance changes if the temperature changes. The thermistors shown in the photographs have **negative temperature coefficients**. This means that their resistance **decreases** if the temperature **rises**.

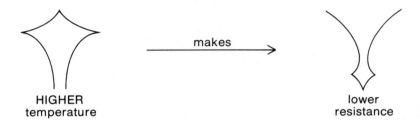

HIGHER temperature   makes   lower resistance

The resistance of a VA1066S changes from about 5000 Ω at 25 °C to 200 Ω at 150 °C.

Variable resistor

When the spindle rotates, the slider turns with it. If the spindle rotates clockwise, the resistance between a and b **increases** and the resistance between b and c **decreases**.

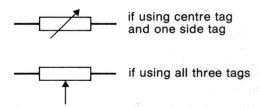

if using centre tag and one side tag

if using all three tags

The symbols for a variable resistor

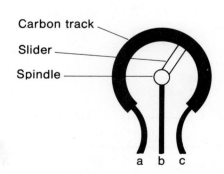

Carbon track

Slider

Spindle

a   b   c

Sensors and information – a summary

Sensor	non-electrical information	becomes	electronic information
Light-dependent resistor	a change of light level	becomes	a change of resistance
Thermistor	a change of temperature	becomes	a change of resistance
Switch	a change of pressure	becomes	a change of resistance
Variable resistor	rotation of the spindle	becomes	a change of resistance

Input voltage unit

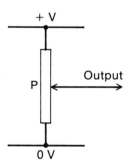

An input voltage unit contains a variable resistor connected so that all three tags are used. P is wherever the slider is touching the carbon track. If the slider is halfway round, the output voltage is half of the supply voltage. Turning the spindle from this position raises or lowers the output voltage.

You normally fix a knob on the end of the spindle. If instead of this you fix a long arm to it, the spindle could be turned by a small force acting at the end of the arm.

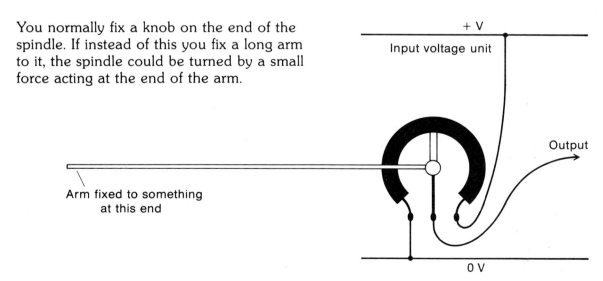

This arrangement is used in Jaguar cars as a throttle position sensor. It feeds information into the engine management system (see p. 80).

How a light sensing unit works

A sensor changes the pattern of incoming information into a pattern of resistance changes. To change the resistance pattern into a voltage pattern the sensor has to be put with a resistor. The circuit is like a cliff that goes down to the sea in just two steps. The width of the ledge makes no difference to the heights of the steps.

If R_1 and R_2 have the same resistance, the voltage at P is half of the positive line voltage.

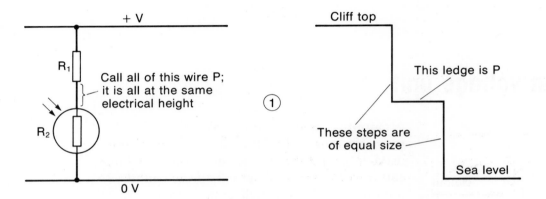

With more light shining on the LDR its resistance is less than it was. R_2's resistance is now less than R_1's so the voltage at P is less than half of the positive line voltage.

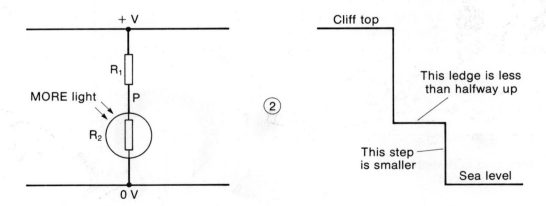

The important point is that **the voltage pattern at P follows the pattern of light levels**. P is the output terminal of the unit.

The LDR's resistance is the same as in ② but R_1's resistance has been increased. (R_1 could be a variable resistor.) The voltage at P is lower than in ②.

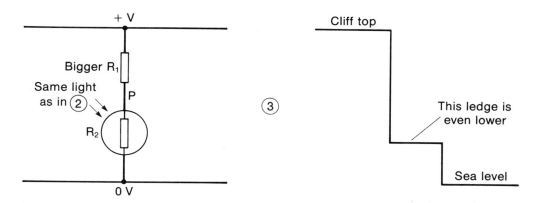

With the LDR in darkness its resistance could be millions of ohms. P would be nearly at positive line voltage.

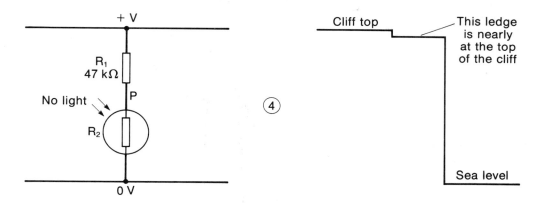

Compared with ④, the positions of the LDR and the resistor have been reversed.

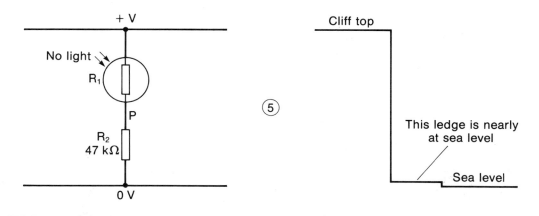

Standard input units for pressure, temperature and light

The standard arrangement of sensor and resistor is to have the sensor in the R_1 position.

If R_1 is a switch, pressure (big enough to close the switch) makes the output voltage high.

If R_1 is a thermistor, high temperature makes the output voltage high.

If R_1 is an LDR, high light level makes the output voltage high.

Pages 148 and 149 explain why this is the case.

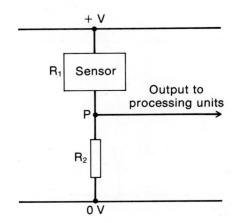

Using LDRs and thermistors to control gates

For perfect switching action and minimum drain of supply current a gate's input voltages should be high (i.e. **positive** line voltage) or low (i.e. **negative** line voltage). However, in simple applications it is possible to use LDRs and thermistors to control gates directly.

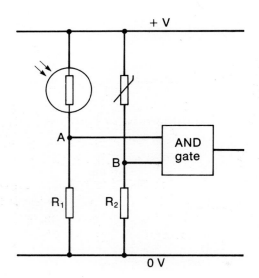

The output of the AND gate will be high if A is high AND B is high. In practice having each of the inputs at just over half of the supply voltage is enough to produce a high output. Therefore the output of this gate is high if the LDR's resistance is less than R_1's resistance AND the thermistor's resistance is less than R_2's resistance.

Using an op-amp as a comparator

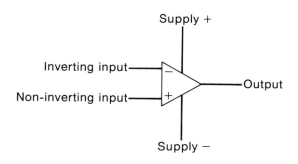

This is the symbol for an **operational amplifier** (**op-amp** for short). Its output is high or low depending upon which input has the higher voltage.

If the + input has a higher voltage than the − input, the output voltage is high.

If the − input has a higher voltage than the + input, the output voltage is low.

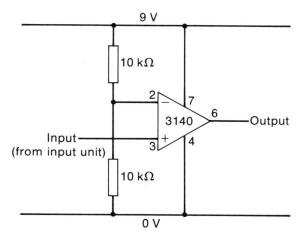

In this **comparator circuit**, pin 2 is at 4.5 V (because the two equal resistors divide up the supply voltage in two equal steps).

If the input voltage is higher than 4.5 V, the output is high.

If the input voltage is lower than 4.5 V, the output is close to 0 V.

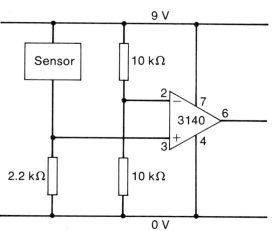

Here again pin 2 is at 4.5 V.

If the resistance of the sensor is less than 2.2 kΩ, the pin 3 voltage is higher than 4.5 V. Pin 3 is at a higher voltage than pin 2 so the output is high.

If the resistance of the sensor is bigger than 2.2 kΩ, the pin 3 voltage is lower than 4.5 V. Pin 3 is at a lower voltage than pin 2 so the output is close to 0 V.

A 3140 is an 8-pin IC package, like a 555. In some circuits it can be replaced by a 741, which is a lot cheaper. However, the output voltage of a 741 only goes down to 2 V as its low value. This is not low enough to turn off a transistor.

Using an op-amp as an amplifier

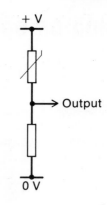

Sometimes an input unit produces a voltage change which is too small to affect the next part of the system.

Example 1 You may need a very sensitive temperature-sensing device. **Very sensitive** means that it **shows very small changes** of temperature.

If the temperature of the thermistor changes by just 1°C, the output voltage may change by too little to affect the next part of the system.

Example 2 A carbon microphone can be used like the other sensors. Its resistance is about 1 kΩ, but a sound wave makes the resistance fluctuate.

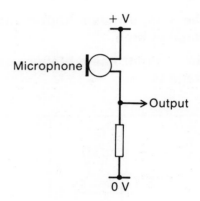

With a quiet sound, the output voltage may change by too little to affect the next part of the system.

If the voltage change is too small, it must be **amplified**. Amplified means 'made bigger'.

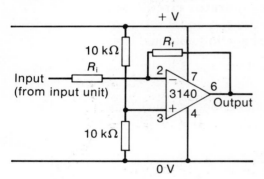

In this circuit the output voltage follows the same pattern as the input voltage. However, it could be bigger or smaller, depending upon the ratio of R_f to R_i.

Inverting amplifier

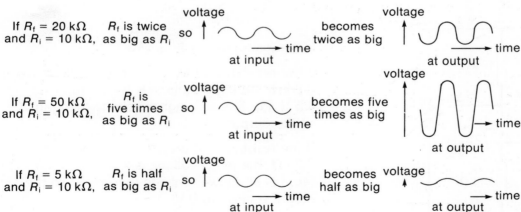

If $R_f = 20$ kΩ and $R_i = 10$ kΩ, R_f is twice as big as R_i so becomes twice as big

If $R_f = 50$ kΩ and $R_i = 10$ kΩ, R_f is five times as big as R_i so becomes five times as big

If $R_f = 5$ kΩ and $R_i = 10$ kΩ, R_f is half as big as R_i so becomes half as big

Normally the resistors are chosen to make the output voltage bigger than the input voltage. This is why the circuit is called an **amplifier**.

Notice also that the output voltage pattern seems to be upside-down. It goes down when the input voltage goes up. This is why the circuit's full name is an **inverting amplifier**.

The number of times the output is bigger than the input is called the **gain**.

An electrical thermometer

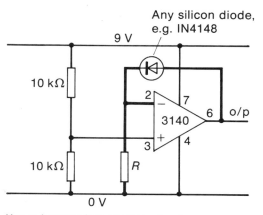

Linear temperature sensing circuit

Any silicon diode, e.g. IN4148

9 V

10 kΩ

10 kΩ

R

3140

2

7

3

6 o/p

4

0 V

The output voltage of this circuit is linearly related to the temperature of the diode. This means that a graph of output voltage against temperature would be a straight line.

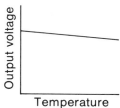

With $R = 100$ kΩ the output voltage falls by about 40 mV (=0.04 V) when you hold the diode firmly between a finger and thumb.

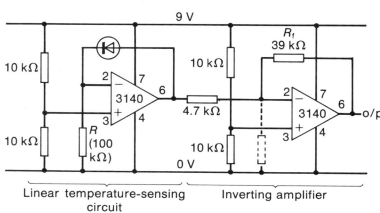

Linear temperature-sensing circuit

Inverting amplifier

This plus a testmeter or chart recorder connected to measure the output voltage equals a complete thermometer

The inverting amplifier does two useful jobs in this situation.
(1)   It ensures that the final output voltage **rises** when the temperature rises.
(2)   It makes the final changes of voltage big enough to be measured accurately by an ordinary testmeter.

You can increase the sensitivity of the thermometer by increasing the value of R_f.

You can alter the range over which temperature measurements can be made by adding the dashed resistor. It will have to be a few hundred kilohms and you may want to change R to 47 kΩ.

Typical test data:
Voltage at pin 2 = voltage at pin 3 = 4.5 V for both ICs.
With $R = 100$ kΩ, output voltage of the sensing unit is about 5 V.

How the sensing unit works

1   The current flowing through $R = \dfrac{4.5 \text{ V}}{100 \text{ k}\Omega}$. This does not change when the diode is heated.

2   The diode is in series with R, therefore it carries the same fixed current.
3   When a diode with a fixed current flowing through it is heated, the voltage drop across the diode decreases linearly with temperature.
4   Since pin 2 of the IC is at a fixed voltage level, the voltage at pin 6 must decrease linearly with temperature.

Questions

1 **(a)** If the temperature of a thermistor changes, what property of the thermistor changes?
   (b) If the temperature rises, what happens to this property?

2 **(a)** If the amount of light on an LDR changes, what property of the LDR changes?
   (b) If the light level rises, what happens to this property?

3 **(a)** If all the data shown on the diagram is correct, what is the resistance of the thermistor?

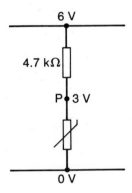

   (b) If the spray from an aerosol freezer is directed at the thermistor its temperature can be lowered to about −60 °C. What will happen to:
    (i) its resistance,
    (ii) the voltage at P?

4 **(a)** If all the data shown on the diagram is correct, what do you think is the resistance of the thermistor?

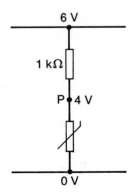

(b) Suppose the thermistor were on very long leads so that it was inside an oven. If the oven were switched on and then left on at the same temperature setting for an hour, what would happen to:
   (i) the resistance of the thermistor,
   (ii) the voltage at P?

5 **(a)** What is a transducer?
   (b) What energy transformation takes place in a:
    (i) microphone,
    (ii) loudspeaker,
    (iii) buzzer?

6 With your thumb held firmly on the top surface of an LDR the resistance of the LDR fluctuates **very** slightly but at a steady rate, something like this:

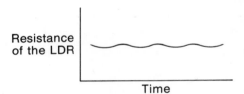

(a) What do you think causes the resistance fluctuation?

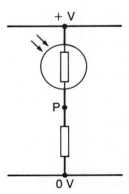

(b) If the LDR were connected like this, what would be happening at P?
(c) Suggest a possible use for this effect, and if possible suggest what other modules would be required in a full electronic system.

Before attempting questions 7 to 10, read 'Using LDRs and thermistors to control gates' which is on p. 150.

7 For the buzzer to be on,
  (a) what must be the resistance of LDR_1 and what must be the resistance of LDR_2?
  (b) what lighting conditions must apply?

8 For the buzzer to be on,
  (a) what must be the resistance of LDR_1 and what must be the resistance of LDR_2?
  (b) what lighting conditions must apply?

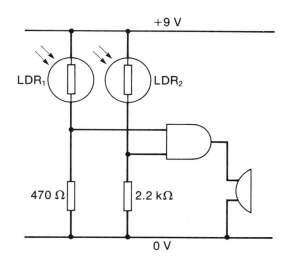

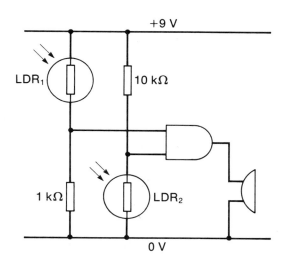

9 Under what circumstances will the buzzer be on?

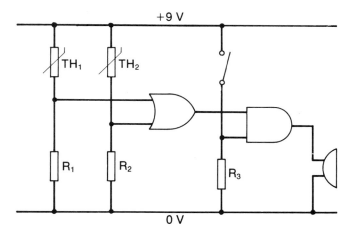

10 Draw the circuit diagram of a system that will turn a buzzer on if it is both cold and dark, or if a switch is closed.

11 Imagine a spring fixed at the top end and supporting an object at the bottom. If you pull the object further down and let go, it oscillates up and down for quite a long time with the oscillations gradually dying away.

Work out the details of a technique whereby the oscillations of the mass will control the same pattern of oscillations of the pointer of a testmeter. Your answer should include:

(a) a full-page, carefully-drawn diagram showing the mechanical and electrical arrangements,

(b) neat and detailed labelling to emphasise points of technique,

(c) a description of any details that are not made clear by the labelled diagram.

12 A circular disc could have slots cut into it. Different numbers of slots could be covered, and a motor could make the disc rotate at a steady speed.

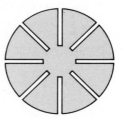

How could you use such a disc to see how the resistance of an LDR varied with the amount of light that reached the LDR? Your answer should include:

(a) a good diagram of the full arrangement,

(b) the procedure for making the measurements,

(c) a data table showing the column headings.

12 Transistor switch: transducer driver

Gate circuits cannot provide enough power to drive water pumps, solenoid bolts, bright lights and loud alarms. A circuit is needed which allows the output device to receive the power it needs **from the power supply** while still being under the control of the gate system. A circuit that does this job is called a **transducer driver**.

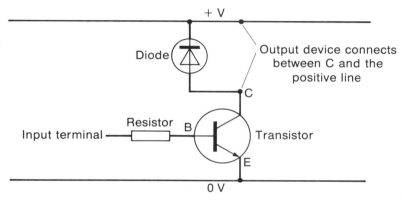

Transducer driver circuit (transmitter switching circuit)

The simplest transducer driver circuit uses a transistor, a resistor and a diode.

The rest of this chapter shows how it works and how it can be used.

Transistors

A transistor has three leads which are connected to a single crystal. In most transistors the crystal is made of almost pure silicon. The crystal has tiny amounts of other elements added to it to form three regions which are called the **collector**, the **base** and the **emitter**.

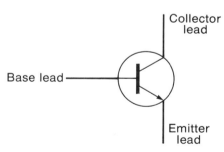

The symbol for a transistor

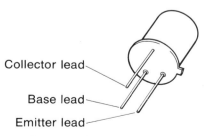

A 2N3053 or BFY51 transistor

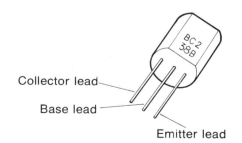

A BC238 transistor

Studying transistor switching action

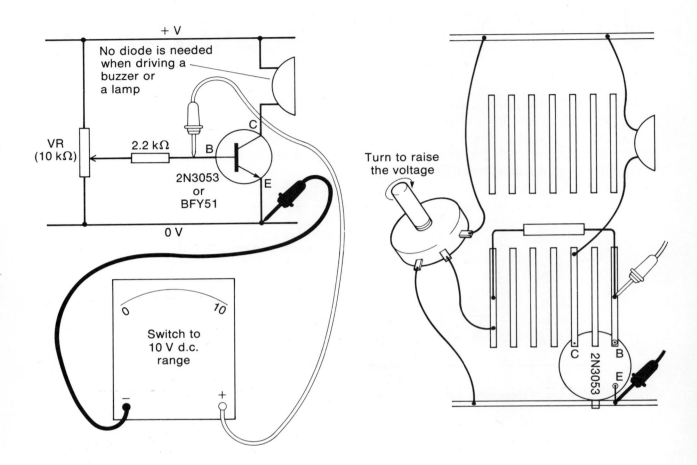

The illustrations above show a circuit diagram and prototype board layout for studying transistor switching action. Notice which way the transistor fits. Its leads should not be crossed over. They only need to be parted a little. You end up with the collector on the left and the base on the right.

1 Start with the spindle of VR turned fully anticlockwise so that the voltage at B is zero. The buzzer is silent.

2 Turn the spindle **slowly** clockwise. The voltage at B rises, but the buzzer remains silent while the voltage at B is below 0.6 V.

3 When the voltage at B reaches about 0.6 V the buzzer turns on.

4 As you continue to turn the spindle round, the voltage at B remains at 0.6 V (or very slightly higher) and the buzzer remains on.

5 If you transfer the meter positive connection to C instead of B you find that:
    (a) while the buzzer is off, C is at positive line voltage,
    (b) when the buzzer is on, C is 0 V volts (or very close to 0 V).

Summary of transistor switching action

1 If the input voltage is low, the transistor behaves like an open switch.

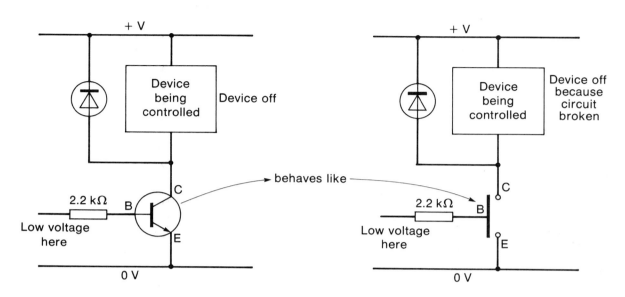

2 If the input voltage is high, the transistor behaves like a closed switch.

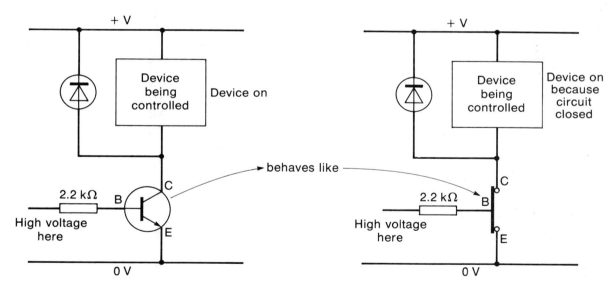

The **base resistor** is needed so that the input voltage can be high (i.e. positive line voltage) without the base voltage going much over 0.6 V. Or you could think of it as preventing the **base current** from becoming too big.

The **diode** is needed to prevent damage to the transistor when the output device switches off. Motors and relay coils can momentarily generate over 100 V when they switch off.

A diode is not needed with output devices which do not produce strong magnetic fields, such as lamps and buzzers.

Transducer driver action

When a transistor is acting like a closed switch there might be a big current flowing through the device that is being controlled. However, the current flowing at the input is **always** tiny.

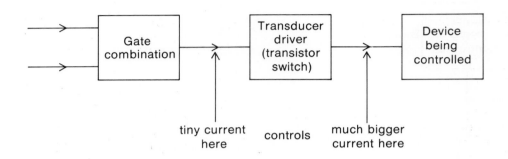

tiny current   controls   much bigger
here   current here

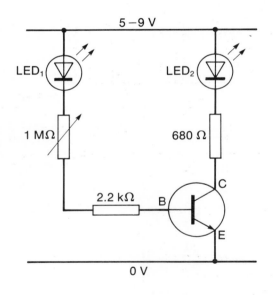

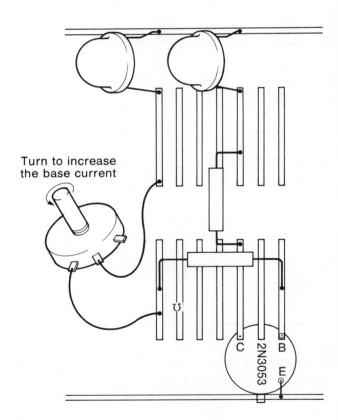

Turn to increase
the base current

**Circuit diagram and prototype board layout
for demonstrating transducer driver action**

The variable resistor controls the base current. You will find that:
- LED$_2$ is much brighter than LED$_1$, showing that the output (**collector**) current is much bigger than the input (**base**) current,
- by controlling the **base** current you also control the **collector** current.

Light-dependent switches

A reminder

If the voltage at B is less than 0.6 V, the transistor behaves like an open switch. The buzzer is off.

If the voltage at B is 0.6 V or slightly higher, the transistor behaves like a closed switch. The buzzer is on.

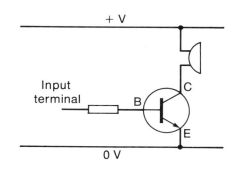

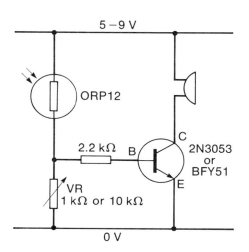

The circuit diagram for a light-dependent switch

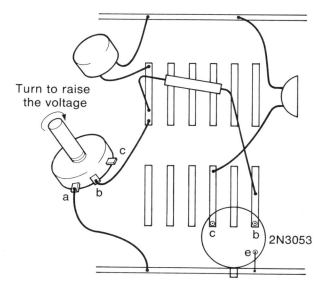

The prototype board layout for a light-dependent switch

The illustrations above show a circuit diagram and prototype board layout for studying the operation of a light-dependent switch.

1 Start with the spindle turned so that VR has its maximum resistance (fully clockwise if you are using tags a and b, fully anticlockwise if you are using b and c). If the LDR is receiving normal daylight the buzzer should be on.

2 You should be able to turn the buzzer off in two ways:
EITHER by covering the LDR so that its resistance increases,
OR by reducing the resistance of VR.

3 With the LDR receiving normal daylight, adjust VR so that the buzzer is on, but only just.

Partially shade the LDR so that the buzzer goes off. Keep it partially shaded and check that you can get it to come on again by adjusting VR. By **adjusting VR** you can make the buzzer switch on or off at **different light levels**.

How the circuit works

With the LDR in darkness, its resistance is very big:
- so the voltage at B is below 0.6 V,
- so the transistor behaves like an open switch,
- so the buzzer is off.

With enough light on the LDR, its resistance is small:
- so the voltage at B is 0.6 V or slightly more,
- so the transistor behaves like a closed switch,
- so the buzzer is on.

In this circuit the positions of the LDR and the variable resistor have been reversed (and a VR of higher maximum resistance is used). The explanation of how the circuit works follows the same steps as the preceding circuit.

With the LDR in darkness, its resistance is
. . .
- so the voltage at B is . . .
- so the transistor . . .
- so the buzzer is . . .

With enough light on the LDR, its resistance is . . .
- so the voltage at B is . . .
- so the transistor . . .
- so the buzzer is . . .

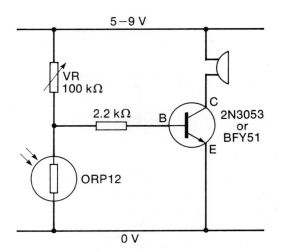

Temperature-dependent switches

If the thermistor is cold enough, its resistance is big:
- so the voltage at B is below 0.6 V,
- so the transistor behaves like an open switch,
- so the buzzer is off.

If the thermistor is hot enough, its resistance is small:
- so the voltage at B is 0.6 V or just above,
- so the transistor behaves like a closed switch,
- so the buzzer is on.

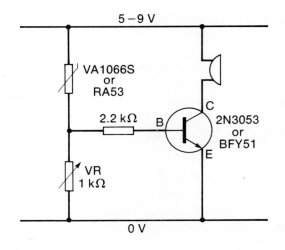

If the thermistor is cold enough, its resistance
is ...
- so the voltage at B is ...
- so the transistor ...
- so the buzzer is ...

If the thermistor is hot enough ...
- so the voltage at B is ...
- so the transistor ...
- so the buzzer is ...

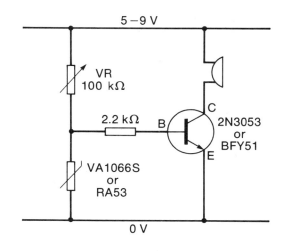

A delayed-action switch

If the switch is closed, P and B are at 0 V and
the buzzer is off. If the switch is opened, the
voltages at P and B rise steadily as the
capacitor charges up. Eventually the voltage
at B reaches 0.6 V and the buzzer turns on.
There is a delay between opening the switch
and the buzzer coming on. The delay time
can be increased by using a bigger resistance
value for R_1 or by using a bigger capacitor.

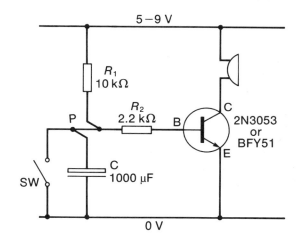

MOSFETs

MOSFET stands for metal-oxide-silicon field-effect-transistor.

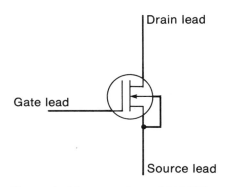

The symbol for an n-channel MOSFET

MOSFETs cost more than ordinary transistors
but they are excellent transducer drivers.

A large current flowing between the drain
and the source can be controlled by the
voltage at the gate. Virtually no current flows
along the gate lead.

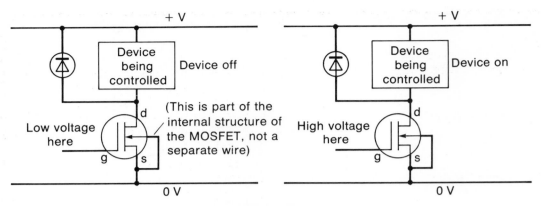

MOSFET transducer driver circuit

Note 1 The output terminal of the final logic gate or op-amp can be connected directly to the gate of the MOSFET.

2 The turn-on voltage for an MPT3055A is about 4.5 V, compared with 0.6 V for ordinary transistors.

An MPT3055A will switch up to 12 A.

An MPT3055A is supplied with a heatsink mounting kit. This usually includes a small bolt which fits through the hole, and an insulating washer.

For currents below 2 A no heatsink is needed. For currents between 2 and 4 A a 19°C/W heatsink will prevent overheating.

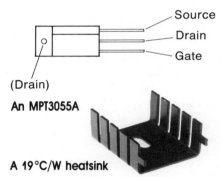

An MPT3055A

A 19°C/W heatsink

Warning MOSFETs are highly sensitive to static electricity. Do not touch the pins of a MOSFET with your hands or your clothes.

Clothes and skin are quite good insulators. Parts of them might have enough static charge to damage a MOSFET.

A MOSFET is supplied in a conducting package. Remove it from the package with pliers, and use pliers if you want to bend the leads. Always return it to its package when you are not using it.

If you heed this warning, you can use MOSFETs safely in prototype board layouts and soldered circuits.

When p-channel and n-channel types are connected like this, they form a circuit in which one transistor is off when the other one is on, and vice versa. Each transistor is called the **complement** of the other.

Arrangements based on this idea are used in complementary metal-oxide-silicon (CMOS) ICs.

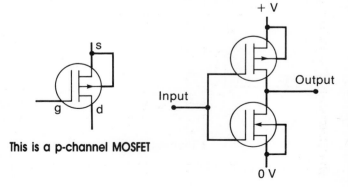

This is a p-channel MOSFET

Questions

1 What is the function of a transducer driver?

2

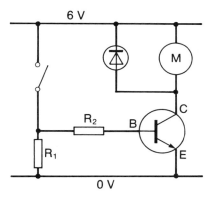

(a) What does the direction of this arrow tell you?

(b) The power requirement of the motor is much greater than the power output of the gate. Where does the power to drive the motor come from?

3

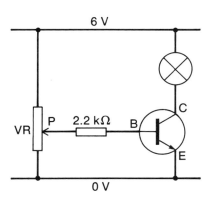

(a) In this circuit, which component is the diode protecting?

(b) If the diode were omitted, when would damage occur?

(c) Why is R_2 needed?

4

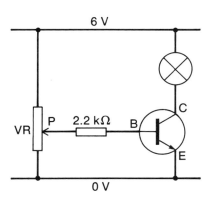

The slider of the potential divider (VR) starts at the negative-line end of the VR so that P is at 0 V. If the slider is slowly moved towards the positive-line end of the VR, describe the effect on:

(a) the voltage at P,
(b) the voltage at B,
(c) the voltage at C,
(d) the lamp.

5

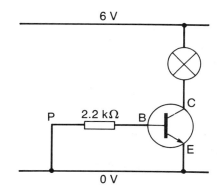

What is the voltage at:
(a) P,   (b) B,   (c) C?

6

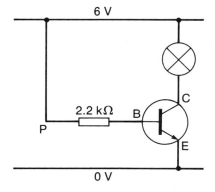

What is the voltage at:
(a) P,   (b) B,   (c) C?

7

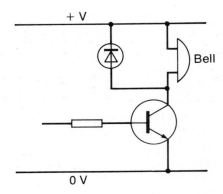

Copy the diagram with the following modifications.
- Change the bell to a buzzer and omit the diode.
- Add a switch and a resistor to control the input voltage so that the input voltage is zero only when the switch is closed.

9

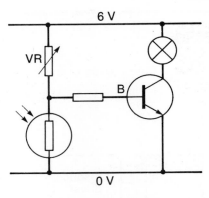

(a) Explain why the lamp should be on if the LDR is in darkness.

(b) With the LDR receiving normal daylight, VR is adjusted so that B is at 0.5 V and the lamp is off. If you then shine light from a torch on to the LDR, what will happen to the bulb? Why?

8

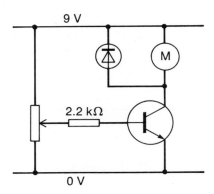

Decide what values of voltage correctly complete these sentences.

(a) To make the motor off, the base voltage must be . . .

(b) When the motor is off, the collector voltage is . . .

(c) To make the motor on, the base voltage must be . . .

(d) When the motor is on, the collector voltage is . . .

10

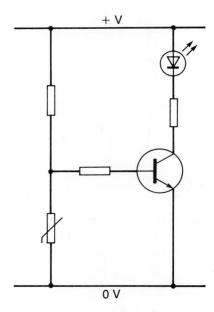

Describe and explain what happens to the LED if the thermistor starts by being hot and then gradually cools.

13 Reed switches, solenoids and relays

Reed switches

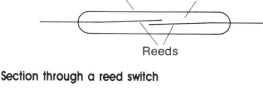

Glass envelope   Inert gas to prevent corrosion

Reeds

Section through a reed switch

The 'reeds' in a reed switch are strips of magnetic alloy.

If a magnet comes close to them, the reeds are magnetised and they move together. The switch is closed, but it will open as soon as the magnet is removed.

A reed switch can be used for switch control of gates (see p. 127).

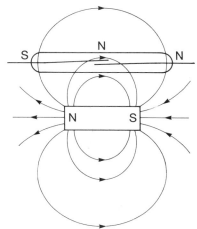

A reed switch within a magnetic field

Reed relays

A reed-operating coil (a **solenoid**) can be used instead of a magnet. The reeds will be magnetised and move together if a big enough current flows through the coil.

The combination of reed switch and reed-operating coil is called a **reed relay**. The circuit diagram shows how a relay can be used to control a motor. The 'switch' that controls the coil could be a transducer driver (i.e. a transistor switch) circuit.

A reed switch in a coil

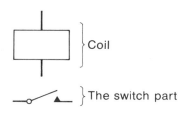

The symbol for a relay

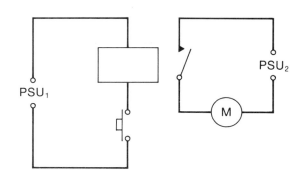

A relay controlling a motor

The advantages of using a relay

1 The output device may need to have a big current flowing through it. The switch contacts can be closed by a small current in the coil circuit. A large current in one circuit is being switched by a small current in a completely separate circuit.

2 The two power supply units can have different voltages. The coil could be operated by a small battery voltage while the switch part controls a mains voltage circuit.

Changeover switches

A stairway lighting system uses **changeover switches** to enable the bulb to be controlled by switches at the top and bottom of the stairs. In the drawing, the upstairs switch has been left in the down position and the downstairs switch has been left in the up position.

Follow the wire from L and see that you can follow an unbroken path back to N. The light will be on but it can be turned off by moving **either** the upstairs switch to the up position **or** the downstairs switch to the down position.

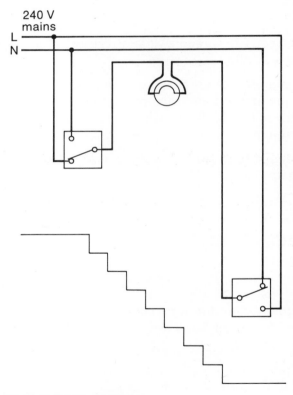

Stairway lighting system

The drawing shows a **changeover reed switch**. When there is no magnetic field present, the reed is connected to the contact labelled NC, which stands for **normally closed**. A magnetic field makes the reed move to the contact labelled NO, which stands for **normally open**.

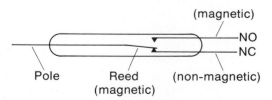

A single-pole double-throw (SPDT) reed switch
(also called a changeover switch)

Controlling a motor

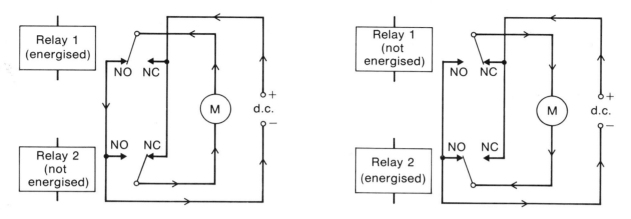

Two changeover relays can control the direction of rotation of a motor as well as whether the motor is on or off. In both of the situations drawn here a current flows through the motor, therefore the motor must be on. However, the **direction** of the current through the motor is different in the two cases so the direction of rotation of the motor must also be different. If neither relay is energised (or both are energised), the motor is **off**.

Electromechanical relays

Reed relays are limited to controlling relatively small currents. Electromechanical relays can be used for controlling much bigger currents.

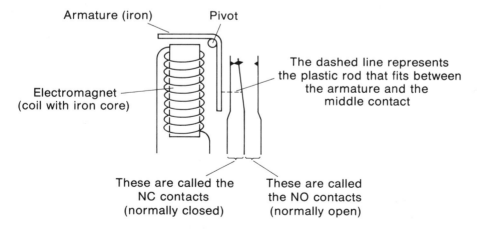

The diagram shows a changeover type of electromechanical relay. When a big enough current flows through the coil, the top of the armature is pulled down to the iron core. The middle contact of the switch is pushed across the gap between the fixed contacts. The NC contacts open and the NO contacts close.

Extra information on selected relays and how to drive them

The relays described here fit across the centre channel of a prototype board, just like IC packages. When used in soldered circuits, they fit into ordinary IC sockets, though the big one is a tight fit and a special socket is available for it. Since none of the relay-terminals need soldering they can be reused as new.

Ultraminiature relay SPDT 2 A

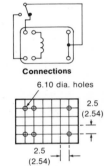

Connections

6.10 dia. holes

2.5 (2.54)

2.5 (2.54)

Pitch/underside view

H: 11.7 mm excl. pins
W: 11.7 mm
D: 16.2 mm

Technical specification

Contact rating	2 A or 12 V max. (60 V A/30 W) (Au/Ag gold clad)
Contact arrangement	Single pole changeover
Coil voltages	6 V or 12 V d.c.
Operating life	5 000 000 no load or 500 000 max. load

This relay is cheap and fits into a 14-pin socket. The coil current is less than 100 mA (Rapid Electronics)

This transducer driver circuit works well in many of the project situations that you are likely to meet. The current in the output device must not exceed 100 mA.

If the single transistor version of the circuit is found to affect the operation of the processing part, or if the output device needs a current greater than 100 mA, use this **darlington pair** arrangement. Choice of the second transistor may depend upon the current needed for the output device. The types shown will work for currents up to 1 A.

If the current to be switched exceeds 1 A, consider using a MOSFET.

Miniature p.c.b. double pole – 5 A

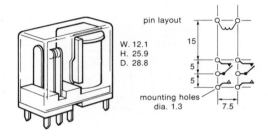

pin layout

W. 12.1
H. 25.9
D. 28.8

15

5

5

mounting holes
dia. 1.3

7.5

Double-pole changeover relays with fine silver contacts rated. 5 A (resistive) at 30 V d.c./250 V a.c. Coil to contact proof voltage 2.5 kV r.m.s. 50 Hz. Max ambient temperature + 55 °C. Mechanical life > 10^7 operations. Electrical life $\geqslant 2 \times 10^5$ operations at max. rated load.

This relay can switch the biggest currents that are likely to be found in school projects. It can also be used to switch mains lighting (RS Components)

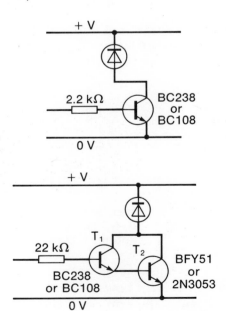

Control of pneumatic valves

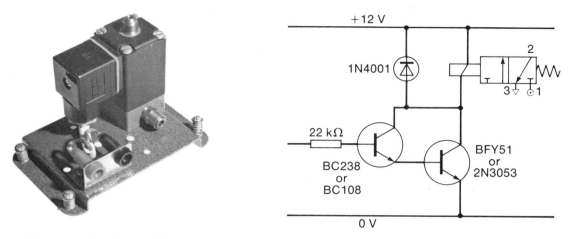

This three-port pneumatic valve is of the type used in many schools' pneumatic kits

It is solenoid-operated and the solenoid needs 12 V, 0.5 A. It can therefore be controlled by the darlington pair arrangement shown, or by either of the relays, or by either of the buffer boxes described in Chapter 3.

Driving an impulse counter

You may want to know how many times a button has been pressed, or a door has been opened, or a light beam has been cut. Use an **impulse counter**. It counts the number of voltage pulses which arrive.

The model shown in the photograph can fit directly onto a prototype board or be used in a final soldered circuit.

It is solenoid-operated and in one version the solenoid needs 12 V, 9 mA. It can therefore be driven by the single transistor version of the transducer driver circuit.

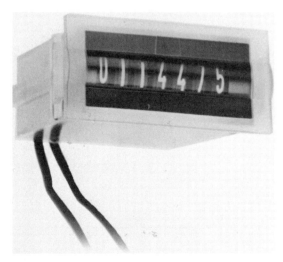

Miniature printed circuit board mounting impulse counter

Questions

1

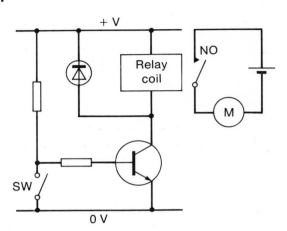

Describe in as much detail as you can what happens:
(a) when the switch, SW, is open,
(b) when SW is closed.

2

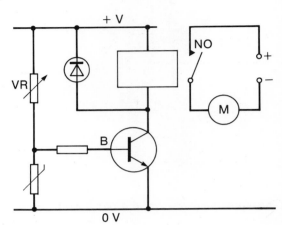

(a) Explain why the motor should be on if the thermistor is cold enough (assuming VR is set to an appropriate value).
(b) To turn the motor off:
  (i) what has to happen to the voltage at B,
  (ii) should the resistance of VR be increased or decreased?
(c) How could the circuit be changed so that the motor came on only when a room became too hot?

3   Under what circumstances will the mains lamp be on?

(The moisture detector has a low resistance when wet and a high resistance when dry.)

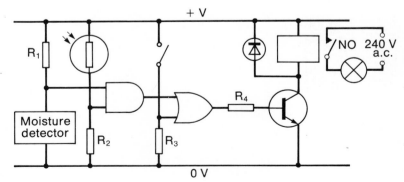

4   Draw the circuit diagram of a system that will turn a pump motor on if the weather is warm enough **and** it is not raining.

5

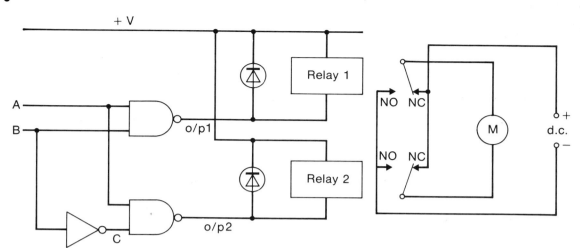

This system consists of the gate combination from question 12 on p. 121 and the motor control circuit from p. 169. Assume that the relay coils require so little power that they can be driven directly by gates. (In practice you would need transducer driver circuits.)

(a) Complete the truth table. (The relays are energised when the voltage controlling them is **low** when they are connected like this.)

(b) Work out from the table which input controls motor on-off and which controls its direction.

A	B	C	o/p 1	o/p 2	Relay 1	Relay 2	State of the motor
low	low						
low	high						
high	low	high	high	low	off	on	on, 'forward'
high	high						

Testing

How to use a testmeter to measure resistance

The resistance scale starts on the right and increases to ∞ on the left. ∞ stands for **infinity**. As the numbers increase they also become closer together, so the pointer must point towards a smallish number if you want an accurate reading.

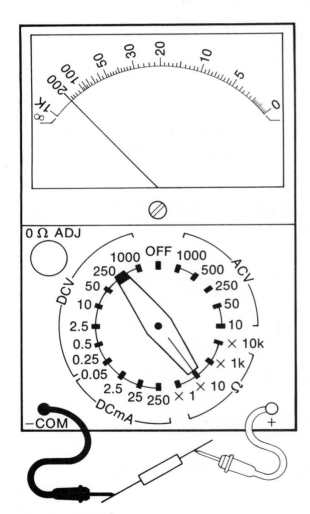

Range: × 10 Ω
Scale reading: 200
Resistance: 200 × 10 Ω
= 2000 Ω

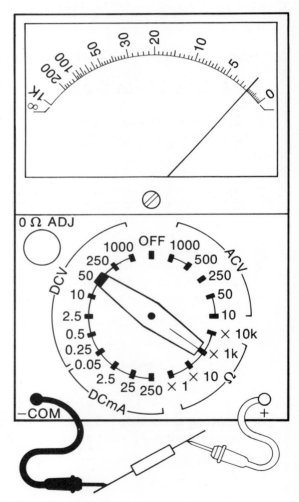

Range: × 1 kΩ
Scale reading: 2.0
Resistance: 2.0 × 1 Ω
= 2.0 kΩ

To prepare the meter for measuring resistance, proceed as follows.

1 Switch to your chosen range.

2 **Set the pointer to zero.** To do this, hold the red and black leads **firmly** together. The pointer should move across the scale to the right. Turn the 0 Ω ADJ knob until the pointer is against the zero mark (which is on the **right** of the ohms scale).

3 Separate the leads as soon as possible to prevent excessive drain on the meter's internal battery.

The meter is now ready for use.

If you find that you made a poor choice of range then change to a different one but **remember to set the pointer to zero every time you change to a different resistance range.**

Some rules on testing

1 **Testing a separate component** This will be a resistance measurement (unless the component is a battery), so switch the testmeter to a resistance range.

2 **Testing a component while it is in a circuit** Make sure that the circuit is switched off if you want to make a resistance measurement.

3 **Tests on a circuit that is switched on** These are likely to be voltage measurements. You cannot make a voltage measurement if the circuit is not switched on. The usual procedure is as follows.

(a) Switch the testmeter to an appropriate voltage range.

(b) Connect testmeter − to the negative line.

(c) Connect testmeter + to wherever you want to know the voltage.

4 **Testing a battery** If your circuit does not work and you suspect the battery, you have to measure the battery voltage twice.

(a) Measure the battery voltage with the battery disconnected from the circuit.

(b) Measure it again while it is powering the circuit.

If the second reading is more than one volt lower than the first, you are probably right to suspect the battery, but it could be that your circuit is shorting the battery.

Analogue versus digital meters

The **analogue meters** shown throughout this book have three advantages for use in a school.

1 They allow you to watch slow changes of voltage and see the pattern of changes.
2 They provide useful practice in reading scales.
3 They are relatively cheap.

However, they have a major limitation. If you use an analogue meter to measure the voltage drop across anything that has a big resistance, the meter alters the voltage that you are trying to measure. **You make an inaccurate measurement**.

Digital meters compared with analogue meters

1 Digital meters can be used to measure the voltage anywhere in a circuit without altering that voltage.
2 They are easier to read.
3 They can be made 'autoranging', like the one in the photograph. This means that you do not have to select a range. The meter's internal circuit automatically selects the best one.

However, **they cannot show a pattern of changes very clearly**.

An autoranging digital multimeter

The picture on the screen of a cathode ray oscilloscope

Cathode ray oscilloscopes are commonly called **oscilloscopes** or **CROs**. An oscilloscope is a voltmeter, like a testmeter that is set to a voltage range. Its main use is to show voltage patterns where the voltage is changing too quickly for an ordinary testmeter to follow.

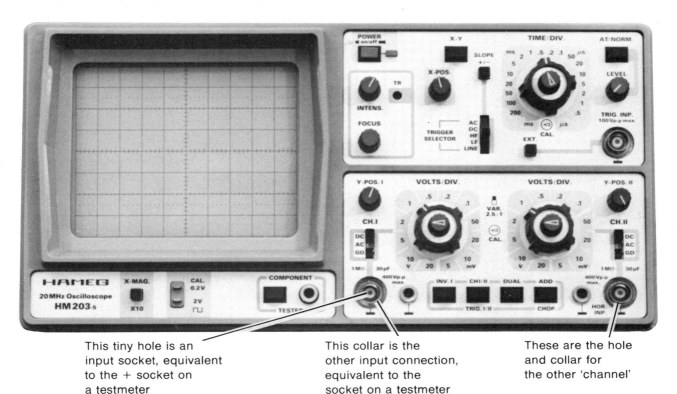

This tiny hole is an input socket, equivalent to the + socket on a testmeter

This collar is the other input connection, equivalent to the socket on a testmeter

These are the hole and collar for the other 'channel'

HAMEG cathode ray oscilloscope, model HM203. This is a double beam oscilloscope. It is like having two voltmeters in a single case. Two patterns can be shown on the screen simultaneously

You have to use two leads to connect it to your circuit, just as you would with an ordinary testmeter. A single coaxial lead contains both of the leads.

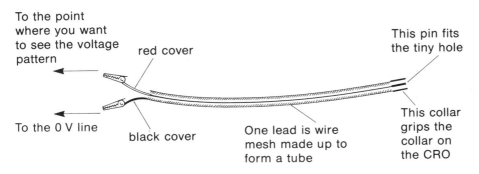

To the point where you want to see the voltage pattern

red cover

This pin fits the tiny hole

To the 0 V line

black cover

One lead is wire mesh made up to form a tube

This collar grips the collar on the CRO

A coaxial lead

An astable produces a 'square wave' voltage pattern.

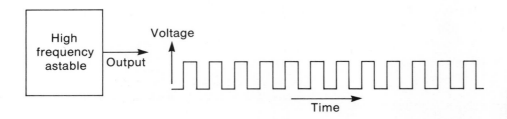

An oscilloscope would give a picture that looked like a snapshot of part of the pattern. It would not appear to be moving or changing.

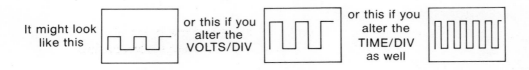

The oscilloscope shows whatever will fit on the screen. This depends upon how you have set the controls.

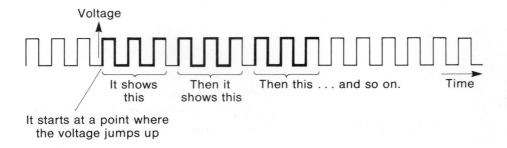

The picture is being renewed continuously. All the 'snapshots' are shown in succession in the same position on the screen.

How different pictures can show the same waveform

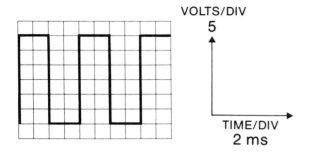

VOLTS/DIV
5

TIME/DIV
2 ms

The overall height of the pattern
   = 6 divisions × 5 volts per division
   = 30 volts.

The time for one cycle
   = 4 divisions × 2 milliseconds per division
   = 8 milliseconds.

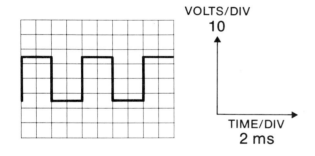

VOLTS/DIV
10

TIME/DIV
2 ms

The overall height of the pattern
   = 3 divisions × 10 volts per division
   = 30 volts.

The time for one cycle
   = 4 divisions × 2 milliseconds per division
   = 8 milliseconds.

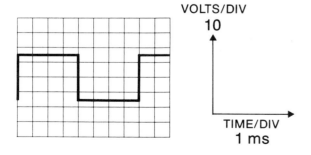

VOLTS/DIV
10

TIME/DIV
1 ms

The overall height of the pattern
   = 3 divisions × 10 volts per division
   = 30 volts.

The time for one cycle
   = 8 divisions × 1 millisecond per division
   = 8 milliseconds.

Questions

1 For each of these testmeters say:
- what range has been selected,
- what the scale reading is,
- what value of resistance or voltage is indicated.

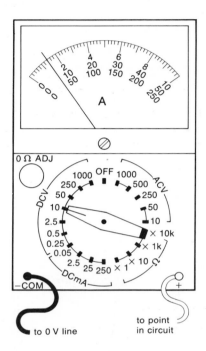

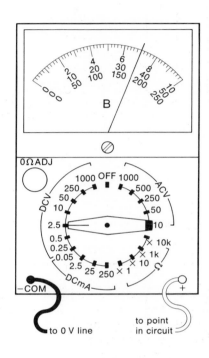

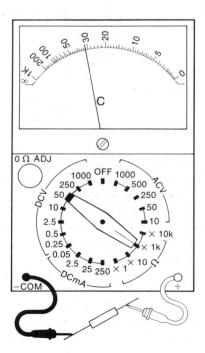

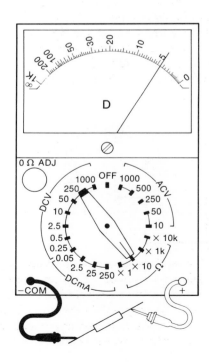

2 A testmeter was used to check the resistance of a resistor. When used on its OHMS × 10 range, the scale reading was 100.

   (a) What is the resistance of the resistor?

   (b) What scale reading should you get if you used the same resistor and the OHMS × 1 range?

3 Suppose that you wanted to test an LDR before putting it in a circuit.

   (a) What LDR behaviour would you have to test for?

   (b) What range would you use?

   (c) Describe precisely how the movement of the pointer would confirm that the LDR was working.

4

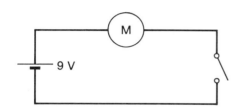

A 9 V battery, a motor and a switch are connected in a simple circuit. When the switch is closed, the motor axle does not move. The fault may be:

   (a) the battery is too run down and incapable of driving the motor,

   (b) a faulty connecting lead.

Describe precisely and in the correct order what you have to do in order to check each possible fault. (You have a testmeter but no spare battery or leads.)

5

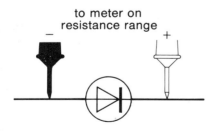

to meter on resistance range

To test a diode you have to measure its resistance 'both ways'. Connected as shown here, the meter should indicate a low resistance, possible about 30 ohms. With the diode reversed, the meter should indicate infinite resistance.

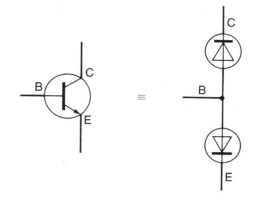

A transistor behaves in some ways as if it were two diodes connected back to back.

Use this information to work out how to **test a transistor** to check that it is not damaged. Write a set of instructions.

6

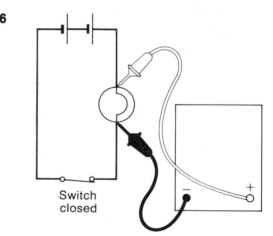

Switch closed

A certain torch contains a bulb powered by two $1\frac{1}{2}$ V cells. When the switch was closed, the bulb stayed off, so a testmeter was connected to it as shown here.

   (a) Which testmeter range should be used?

   (b) What should the reading be if there is nothing wrong with the bulb but the switch is not closing properly?

   (c) What should the reading be if the bulb is blown but everything else is working?

7 Imagine you have built a circuit and it does not work. You first check whether the leads that connect it to the battery are broken.

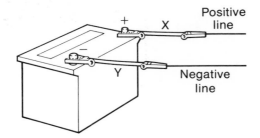

(a) Write down the voltmeter readings to complete the table if lead X is sound and **Y** is **broken**.

Voltmeter connected to	Voltmeter reading
battery **+** and **−**	9 V
battery **+** and **−**ve line	(i)
+ve line and battery **−**	(ii)
+ve line and **−**ve line	(iii)

(b) The broken lead is replaced but the circuit still will not work.

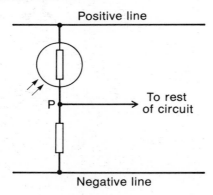

Part of the circuit includes an LDR in this arrangement. To test the LDR you connect a voltmeter between P and the negative line.

How can you use the meter on its 10 V d.c. range to find out if all is well at this part of the circuit? (Say exactly what you have to do and what should happen.)

8 Here are some oscilloscope pictures and the settings of the two main knobs. For each picture calculate:
  (i) the overall height of the pattern,
  (ii) the time for one cycle.

(a)

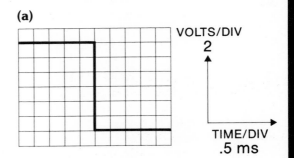

VOLTS/DIV 2
TIME/DIV .5 ms

(b)

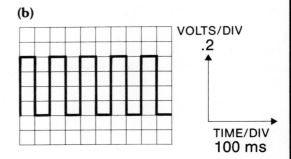

VOLTS/DIV .2
TIME/DIV 100 ms

(c)

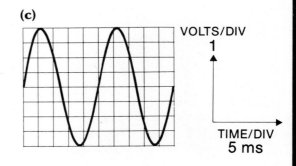

VOLTS/DIV 1
TIME/DIV 5 ms

(d)

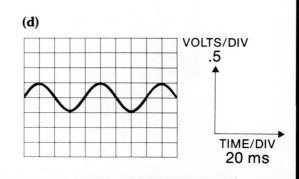

VOLTS/DIV .5
TIME/DIV 20 ms

15 Building a soldered circuit

Using stripboard

A working prototype has to be converted into a soldered circuit that will withstand the hazards of normal use, such as falling to the floor or being knocked about in a drawer. One of the best ways of building a single soldered circuit is to use a piece of **stripboard**.

Stripboard is an insulating board, one side of which is covered with straight copper strips. The board has an array of holes that are 2.5 mm (0.1 inch) apart. The copper strips ensure that all the holes in any row are connected to each other but not connected to the holes in any other row.

The non-copper side of a board with some components in place

The copper side of the same board showing soldered joints

Soldering

You need:
- soldering iron in its stand,
- piece of damp cloth,
- solder.

1   Switch the iron on and wait for it to warm up.

2   If the cloth is dry, wet it, then squeeze out as much water as you can.

3   Hold the handle of the hot iron in your
fingers as you would hold a pen when
writing.

Hold the iron so that the bit is uppermost
and melt **a little** solder on to the bit.

4   Keep the iron still, and with the damp cloth in your other hand wipe
the bit to remove all excess solder. The bit should then be bright and
shiny all over.

The bit is now **tinned** and the iron is ready for use. Replace it in its
stand.

5   Make sure that the wire you are about to
fix comes straight up through the hole.

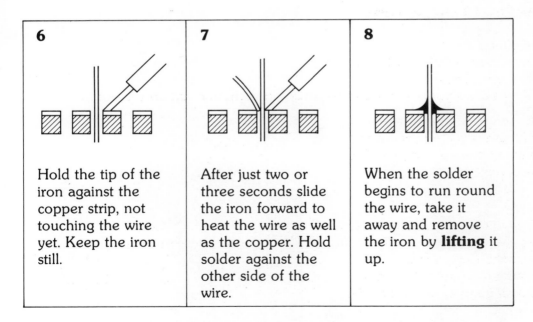

6   Hold the tip of the
iron against the
copper strip, not
touching the wire
yet. Keep the iron
still.

7   After just two or
three seconds slide
the iron forward to
heat the wire as well
as the copper. Hold
solder against the
other side of the
wire.

8   When the solder
begins to run round
the wire, take it
away and remove
the iron by **lifting** it
up.

9   **Wipe the iron to remove excess solder before using it again.**
If you keep the iron free of excess solder, almost anything you do
wrong can easily be put right.

Faults and remedies

 Solder sticks to wire but not to copper. Copper was not hot enough.

Remedy
Heat copper strip again then move iron forward into the solder ball. The solder will run to where things are hottest. Remove the iron.

 Solder sticks to copper but not to wire. Wire was not hot enough.

Remedy
 Turn the iron over and hold the bit against the wire. After a few seconds move it down into the solder then withdraw it along the wire.

Solder has run into the channel between two strips. This must be removed.

Remedy
 Put the tip of the bit into one end of the channel and slide it along to the other end.

Solder spread along strip.

Reason Iron removed by drawing it along the strip, or iron not wiped well enough beforehand.

Solder not shiny.

Probable reason Overheating. Iron left in place too long before solder applied or after solder melted.

Remedy
Clean off and resolder.

Plan of work

1 **Position the tinned copper wires**
   You need:
   - long-nose pliers,
   - tinned copper wire (S.W.G. 22),
   - side cutters (if available).

Each wire should slot exactly into place so that it rests straight and flat on the board.
To achieve this:

(a) Hold a length of wire in pliers and bend it round the edge of the pliers to make a right angle.

(b) Hold the wire against the board so that you can reposition the pliers for the next right angle bend.
Lift the wire away from the board, make the bend, then drop the wire into its holes.

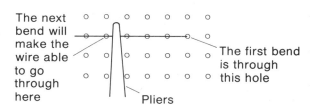

The next bend will make the wire able to go through here

The first bend is through this hole

Pliers

(c) Bend one end under the board to prevent the wire from falling out while you position the other wires.

2 Solder all the wires into place
See p. 184, on soldering.

3 Remove excess wire from every joint
Cut as close as possible to the solder
without cutting into the solder.

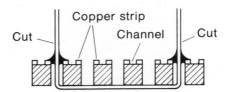

Wire flat against the board
or with a very narrow gap
between it and the board

**4 Use a stripboard cutter to make the cuts shown as X on the
stripboard layout diagram**
Insert the point of the cutter into the hole where the
break is required and rotate the cutter clockwise a few
times until just enough copper has been removed. Blow
or scrape away any loose fragments of copper.

**5 Test each pair of strips to make sure that no solder has
leaked into a channel**
The tiniest solder leak into a channel will
prevent the circuit from working. Some
solder leaks are very difficult to see, so
test all channels as follows:

(a) Switch a testmeter to a resistance
range, $\Omega \times 1$ or $\Omega \times 10$.

(b) Hold the red and black leads firmly
together. The pointer should move
across the scale to the right. Turn
the $0\,\Omega$ ADJ knob until the pointer
is against the zero mark which is on
the **right** of the ohms scale.

(c) Separate the two leads as soon as
possible to prevent excessive drain
on the meter's internal battery.

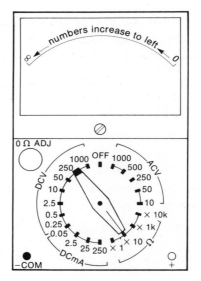

(d) Touch one probe on row 1 of your circuit and the other probe
on row 2. The pointer should remain at the **left** hand side of the
scale, at the ∞ mark (except in unusual cases such as the kitchen
timer circuit where rows 1 and 2 are joined by a wire). ∞ stands
for infinity.

(e) Test rows 2 and 3, then 3 and 4, and so on until you have tested
all the channels.

(f) Clean out any channels that give a zero ohms reading when they
should be giving an ∞ ohms reading. (See 'Faults and remedies'
on p. 185.)

6 Position the terminal pins and solder them

If you are using double-sided pins you can push them through from the non-copper side since you will only make connections from one side of the board.

Terminal pins are relatively thick, so have the iron touching them right from the start. You may even find it better to tilt the iron forward slightly as shown in the right-hand drawing.

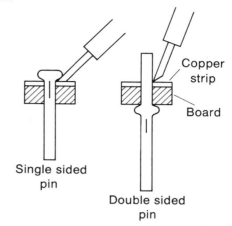

7 Position all resistors that lie flat, solder them and remove excess wire

Make sure that resistors are held against the board while you are soldering them.

8 Position the IC socket(s) and solder the pins

Make sure that the socket is the right way round before you do any soldering.

Also make sure that the socket is held firmly against the board while you are soldering the pins.

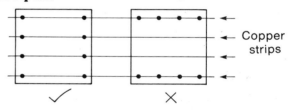

9 Position, solder and remove excess wire from all components that stand on one end

Make sure that these components stand at right angles to the board, that capacitors are the right way round, and that the wire running along the side of a resistor is straight.

10 Using a testmeter on a resistance range as described in item 5, test each break

The pointer should not normally move more than a very small distance from the ∞ position. If it does, clean out the break.

11 Closely inspect every channel

Use a soldering iron to clean out any that do not look perfectly clear.

12 Closely inspect each joint

Try to make each wire or pin move in its hole.
If anything will move, resolder the joint.

13 Tin the tops of the terminal pins on the component side of the board

Heat the end of the pin for a few seconds
before introducing the solder. Take the
iron and the solder away as soon as you
see any solder melt on to the pin.

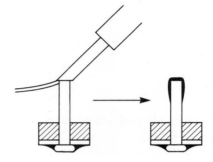

14 Attach all off-board components to the terminal pins

To do this, wrap the appropriate wire tightly round the pin then hold
the iron against the **outside** of the wire. As soon as you see the
solder melt, remove the iron and hold the wire still until the solder
has set.

15 Insert the IC(s) and check that the circuit works as it should

If it does not work:

(a) Disconnect the battery or PSU.

(b) **Carefully** check that every component is in its correct place and
reposition any misplaced component. (You may need help to do
this repositioning.)

(c) With a testmeter on its **10 V d.c.** range, check the battery or PSU
voltage.

(d) Reconnect the battery or PSU to the circuit and measure the
voltage between the +V and 0 V pins of the IC (testmeter + to
+V pin and − to 0 V pin).

(e) If the two voltage measurements are very different, disconnect
the battery or PSU again and look for heat damage to a copper
strip or a solder leak in a channel.

(f) For any other problem you will probably need help to find it if
you are doing your first project.

Examples of circuit layouts

Layout example 1

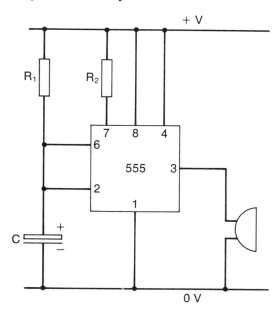

The circuit diagram

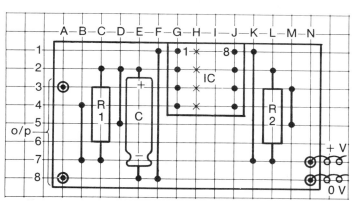

Layout A

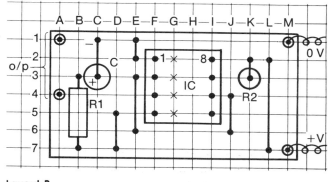

Layout B

The stripboard layout can be drawn on ordinary squared paper, which has 5 mm (0.2 inch) squares. The drawing is then twice as big as the stripboard. This is good because it is easier to draw and to follow the bigger drawing.

You have to imagine that there is a hole wherever two lines of the squared paper cross. Also imagine that the copper strips run **along the numbered rows** so that, for example, all the holes in row 6 are connected to each other.

Answer the following questions for each layout in turn.

1 One end of a connecting wire is connected into hole 5D. Which hole is used for the other end of the wire?

2 Which hole is used for pin 7 of the IC?

3 What do the four X's represent?

4 Which row of holes is used for the negative line?

5 Which row of holes is used for the positive line?

6 Eventually what should be connected to the two terminal pins labelled o/p?

7 How is R_2 mounted?

8 Which two wires and which pieces of copper strip connect pin 2 to pin 6?

9 Is the positive terminal of the capacitor connected to pin 6? If so, how?

10 Is pin 4 connected to pin 8? If so, how?

Layout example 2
An ultrasonic transmitter

C1 and C2 are ordinary capacitors; unlike the electrolytic capacitors that are used in Chapter 3, these capacitors do not have **+** and **−** leads.

VR has been drawn with a T instead of an arrow. This shows that it is a **preset** variable resistor, i.e. one which has to be adjusted with a screwdriver.

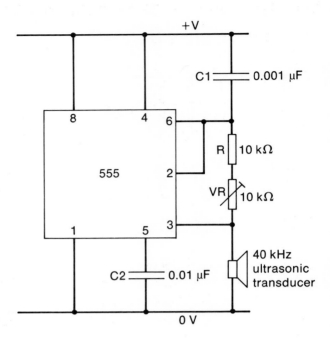

The circuit diagram

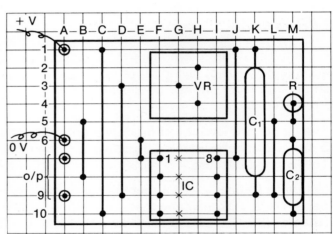

The stripboard layout seen from the side without copper strips

Remember that the copper strips run along the **numbered** rows.

Check your understanding of the layout drawing.

1 Which row of holes is used for the positive line?

2 Which row of holes is used for the negative line?

3 Eventually, what should be connected to the two terminal pins labelled o/p?

4 Which two wires and which pieces of copper strip connect pin 2 to pin 6?

5 Is one end of resistor R connected to pin 2? If so, how?

6 Describe precisely how and where R is mounted.

Layout example 3
Very sensitive light-dependent switching circuit

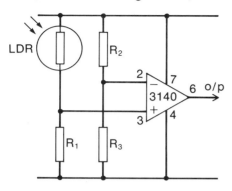

The circuit diagram

 is an operational amplifier (op-amp for short). A 3140 is an 8 pin IC package. It looks just like a 555. Pins 1, 5 and 8 are not used in this circuit.

Design your own stripboard layout.

1 Start by drawing the 3140 on a piece of squared paper. (Remember to think of the copper strips running left to right.)

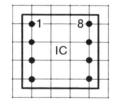

2 Draw crosses for the four cuts that are needed in the copper strips.

3 Choose a negative line. Don't draw it, just remember which line you have chosen.

4 Draw R_1 so that one end connects to the pin 3 row of holes and the other end connects to your negative line.

5 Draw R_3 in an acceptable position so that it makes the right connections.

6 Use a wire to connect pin 4 to your negative line.

7 Choose a positive line and draw R_2 in an acceptable position.

8 Use a wire to connect pin 7 to the positive line.

9 Add two terminal pins for the LDR.

10 Add two terminal pins for the power supply connections.

11 Add a terminal pin to carry the output from pin 6.

12 Add a frame to show the edges of the piece of stripboard that you are using. If necessary move terminal pins so that they are at the ends of rows.

Now start again and produce a layout that looks completely different but which is still correct.

Layout example 4
Alarm controlled by temperature or light level

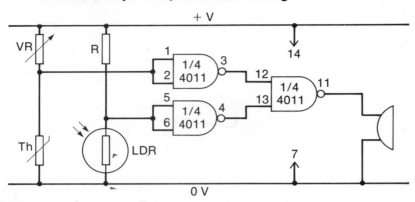

The circuit diagram

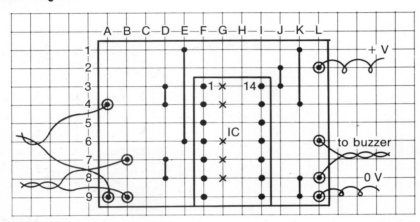

A possible stripboard layout

Check your understanding of the layout diagram.

1 How has pin 4 of the IC been connected to pin 13?

2 How has pin 3 been connected to pin 12?

3 How has pin 7 been connected to the 0 V terminal pin?

4 One of the NAND gates in the 4011 is not used in the circuit. All unused inputs of a CMOS gate should be connected to 0 V or +V. How has this been achieved in this layout?

5 Resistor R is missing in the stripboard layout. Into which holes should it be connected?

6 Which component should be connected to the wires that come from 4A and 9A?

7 Which component should be connected to the wires that come from 7B and 9B?

8 There is an off-board component for which terminal pins have not yet been provided. What is the full name of this component and which holes should be used for the terminal pins?

Layout example 5 Motor controlled by two water level sensors

The circuit includes a bistable (latch) made from two NAND gates. Its operation is similar to that of a NOR gate bistable except that set and reset are normally held high and they work by going low.

The relay is the 5 amp one shown on p. 170.

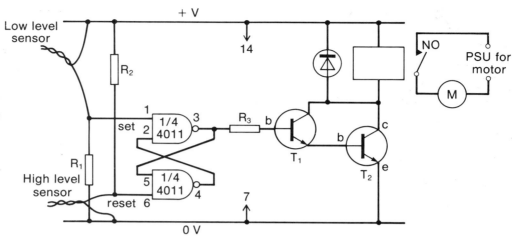

The circuit diagram

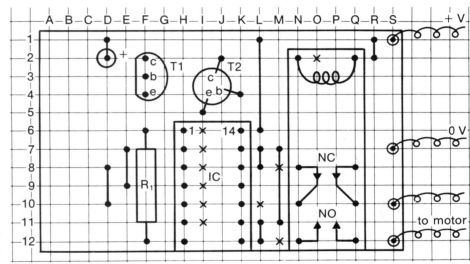

The stripboard layout

Check your understanding of the layout diagram.

1 The emitter of T 1 must be connected to the base of T 2. How has this been achieved?

2 Which wires and which pieces of copper strip connect pin 7 of the 4011 to the 0 V terminal pin?

3 Two of the NAND gates are not used in the circuit. Have all four unused input terminals been connected to 0 V or is another connection needed?

4 Why is it necessary to break the copper strip at 8 M?

5 Into which holes would you connect R_2?

6 Into which holes would you connect R_3?

7 Into which holes would you connect the terminal pins for the low level sensor?

8 Into which holes would you connect the terminal pins for the high level sensor?

9 The emitter of T 2 should be connected to 0 V. Into which holes would you connect the necessary piece of connecting wire?

10 What should be connected to the wire that comes from the terminal pin in 10S?

Layout example 6   Timed motor control

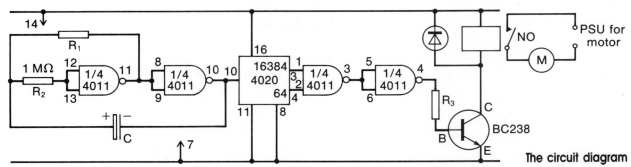

The circuit diagram

There are a number of different ways of making a pulse generator. If a 555 circuit had been used, the system would have used three ICs (leaving half of the 4011 unused). The frequency of the NAND gate pulse generator (astable) circuit is controlled by R_1 and C.

$R_1 = 100\,\text{k}\Omega$ and $C = 4.7\,\mu\text{F}$ gives about one cycle per second.

The relay is the 2 amp one shown on p. 170.

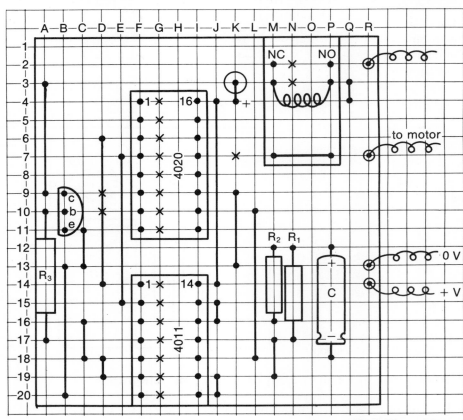

The stripboard layout

Check your understanding of the layout diagram.

1   Which wire and which pieces of copper strip connect pin 7 of the 4011 to the 0 V terminal pin?

2   The p end of the diode has to be connected to the collector of the transistor. How has this been achieved?

3   The n end of the diode has to be connected to the +V terminal pin. How has this been achieved?

4   One end of the relay coil (in 3P) has to be connected to the +V terminal pin. How has this been achieved?

5   What should be connected to the wire that comes from the terminal pin at 2R?

Layout example 7   DIY

Design your own stripboard layout for this circuit.

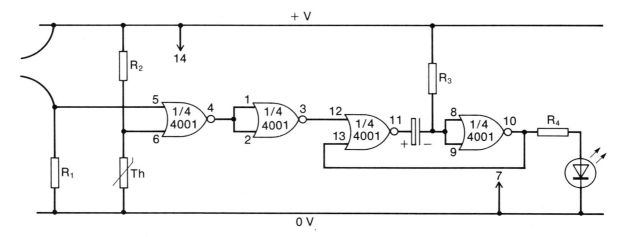

List of suppliers

RS Components catalogue:
  PO Box 99
  Corby
  Northants   NN17 9RS
  Tel: (0536) 201234

Prototype boards illustrated in the text can be obtained directly
from the manufacturers:
  Boss Industrial Mouldings
  James Carter Road
  Mildenhall
  Suffolk   IP28 7DE
  Tel: (0638) 716101

Stepped variable resistors and test meters YN360TR can be
obtained cheaply from Henry's Audio Electronics:
  Cubegate Ltd
  First Floor
  406 Edgeware Road
  London   W2 1ED
  Tel: 01–258–1831

Miniature piezo-electric buzzers that can be driven directly by
CMOS gates can be obtained from:
  Rapid Electronics
  Hill Farm Industrial Estate
  Boxted
  Colchester   CO4 5RD

CONTROL IT buffer boxes and sensors can be obtained from:
  Deltronics
  91 Heol-Y-Parc
  Cefneithin
  Llanelli
  Dyfed   SA14 7DL
  Tel: (0269) 843728

Different versions of CONTROL IT are available, with or
without integral power supply, and with inputs which float low.
RML and Spectrum versions are available.

INTERPACK 2 can be obtained from Griffin and George, or
direct from the manufacturers:
  DCP Microdevelopments
  2 Station Close
  Lingwood
  Norwich   NR13 4AX
  Tel: (0603) 712482

Versions are available for a wide variety of computers.

Electronics units suitable for projects in schools are available
from:

  Omega Electronics
  12 Oxhill Road
  Middle Tysoe
  Warwickshire   CV35 0SX

  Lock International plc
  PO Box OL82
  Neville Street
  Oldham
  Lancs   OL9 6LF

  Unilab
  The Science Park
  Hutton Street
  Furthergate
  Blackburn
  Lancs   BB1 3BT

To make an LED display for INTERPACK 2

(i)   Connect all the Cs to supply positive.
(ii)   Connect all the As to supply negative.
(iii) Connect each B via a series resistor and LED to
       supply negative.

(iv) R value depends upon line voltage, normally
      180 Ω to get a really bright ON if using 5 V.
(v)   You could use the + and − terminals on
      the side of Interpack 2 to power the display. If so,
      use $R = 120$ Ω. The LEDs will not be very bright
      because the supply drops to about 2.7 V when all
      LEDs are on. However, they are bright enough.

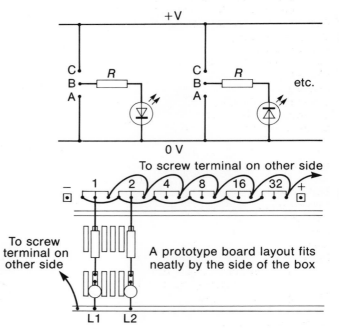

To screw terminal on other side

To screw
terminal on
other side

A prototype board layout fits
neatly by the side of the box

Index